B'NAI B'RITH WOMEN
UNITING JEWISH WOMEN

JOAN KORT
President

Dear Friend,

Thank you for your order. *Mingled Roots* is a result of the action plan B'nai B'rith Women established in 1990, when we resolved to address the controversial issue of interfaith marriage and reach out to interfaith families to help them cope with the challenges of their unique circumstances. Although written for Jewish grandparents with interfaith grandchildren, *Mingled Roots* is a wonderful guide for all Jewish grandparents who want to instill in their grandchildren a sense of pride in being Jewish. The book offers opportunities to teach a child about Jewish traditions and rituals in a sensitive manner, without making either the child or non-Jewish relatives feel uncomfortable. And, perhaps most importantly, *Mingled Roots* aids you in opening a friendly, continuing dialogue within your family on the sensitive topic of religion.

This book is only one aspect of B'nai B'rith Women's campaign to reach out to interfaith families. We regularly sponsor forums for interfaith couples in communities across the nation, and we are conducting studies on Jewish attitudes toward intermarriage in major cities such as Philadelphia and Kansas City. If you enjoy this book, I hope you will consider becoming involved in our interfaith outreach activities in your own community.

And, if you are not already a member of BBW, I strongly urge you to become one. Belonging to BBW is not only a great way to keep up with the latest programs and publications for interfaith families, but it also provides other benefits, such as insurance, the BBW MasterCard, and discounts on Jewish magazines like *Lilith*, *Moment*, and *Noah's Ark*. To become a member, please fill out the enclosed application and return it to this address.

Thank you so much for your interest in *Mingled Roots*. By purchasing this book, you are helping to support our many programs to improve the lives of women and children in the United States, Canada, and Israel.

Sincerely,

Joan Kort
President

D0521521

THE BENEFITS OF BELONGING

Insurance

The BBW-endorsed Long-Term Care Insurance policy helps to ensure financial help for you and your family if a debilitating illness strikes. Call Rollins Burdick Hunter, the insurance administrator, at **1-800-635-9171** for information and a personalized quote.

Magazine Subscription Discounts

Discounts on *Lilith, Moment,* and *Noah's Ark* help keep you in touch with Jewish issues -- and save you up to 55% off regular subscription prices! Call **202-857-1325** for subscription information.

Travel Benefits

Join with women from across North America to celebrate the 50th anniversary of the Residential Treatment Center and the 45th anniversary of the State of Israel. To learn more about the Israel Mission and other meetings, call **202-857-1325**.

BBW Gifts

Coffee mugs, tote bags, and sweatshirts emblazoned with the BBW logo, as well as attractive greeting cards, make great gifts and show pride in your organization. Use the order form in the Resource Catalog for Leaders or call Central Services at **202-857-1315** for further information.

Long-Distance Discounts

The Members Long-Distance Advantage Program makes it possible for you to save 10% off on all your long-distance calls. And each call you make helps BBW automatically, since BBW receives royalties that translate into added support for our programs. Call **1-800-888-8940**, 24 hours a day, to start saving right away!

BBW MasterCard

Take credit for being a B'nai B'rith Women member -- sign up for the BBW MasterCard. You'll have the satisfaction of knowing that with each purchase you make, you are supporting BBW programs. Call **1-800-847-7378** to apply.

B'NAI B'RITH WOMEN

UNITING JEWISH WOMEN

Please reproduce this page in your chapter bulletin.

Introducing

MINGLED ROOTS: A GUIDE FOR JEWISH GRANDPARENTS OF INTERFAITH GRANDCHILDEN

Commissioned by B'nai B'rith Women, Mingled Roots is a loving 'how-to,' offering specific suggestions to help grandparents share their Jewish heritage with their grandchilden.

Author Sunie Levin wrote this book for all Jewish grandparents seeking to build a stronger relationship with their grandchildren.

"...a sensitive, practical guide...Levin's tone [is] familiar, warmand loving...it is clear that she truly understands the ins and outs of grandparenting."

Leslie Katz
Northern California Jewish Bulletin

"The best way to teach is, of course, by example, by letting children see that their grandparent is someone to be proud of because of the way he lives and treats others. The only real way to teach your grandchild to be a mensch is to be one yourself."
From *Mingle Roots: A Guide for Jewish Grandparents of Interfaith Grandchildren*

"...a handy tool for anyone who's had trouble talking about religion with a child...[it] has some wonderful ideas."

Stephen Ben-Allen
Rhode Island Jewish Herald

To order your copy of *Mingled Roots: a Guide for Jewish Grandparents of Interfaith Grandchildren*, mail a check or money order, according to the following schedule, made payable to **B'nai B'rith Women, Inc.**, with the completed form.:

1 - 9 copies	$13.95 each
10 - 25 copies	$10.00 each
26 - 50 copies	$ 9.50 each

For quanities over 50 call (202) 857-1315

Name: _____

Address: _____

City, State, Zip _____

Return to:
B'nai B'rith Women
1828 L Street, N.W., Suite 250
Washington, D.C. 20036

To order using Visa or MasterCard, Call **1-800-229-4664**

MINGLED ROOTS

A Guide for Jewish Grandparents of Interfaith Grandchildren

SUNIE LEVIN
Illustrated by Margaret Scott

B'NAI B'RITH WOMEN
1828 L STREET, N.W., SUITE 250
WASHINGTON, D.C. 20036

A gift from

TEMPLE BETH AM
Seattle

This book is lovingly dedicated to my grandchildren.

Amanda

Danny

David

Jillian

Megan

Rachel

Sean

PROLOGUE

In 1989, B'nai B'rith Women (BBW) commissioned a landmark study to examine the attitudes of Jewish women towards intermarriage. The survey revealed that BBW members would rather see their adult children marry a non-Jew than not marry at all; that they fervently want their grandchildren to be raised as Jews; and that they were clearly dissatisfied with the Jewish community's response to intermarriage.

Recognizing a call to action, B'nai B'rith Women created an interfaith marriage task force and set about addressing the issue with conferences, seminars, and other programs throughout the country. The response to these interfaith activities confirmed the tremendous need for more outreach from the Jewish community. In addition, it revealed a dearth of information and/or support for grandparents, the generation 'once removed' in most interfaith situations.

How can Jewish grandparents transmit family traditions and heritage to their interfaith grandchildren without alienating non-Jewish sons or daughters-in law? For BBW that question demanded an answer, because passing Jewish tradition on to the next generation is central to our mission.

And so, *Mingled Roots* was commissioned—to serve as a loving 'how-to,' offering specific suggestions to help grandparents share their Jewish heritage in ways that would not threaten their intermarried children. Author Sunie Levin has, we feel, created a warm and caring guide based on her own experience as an educator and as a Jewish grandmother.

For B'nai B'rith Women, the publishing of *Mingled Roots* underscores its commitment to serve as a connecting ethnic and cultural link for interfaith families—helping them communicate openly and lovingly. The result, we hope, will be to nurture and to strengthen Jewish identity and to insure the survival of Jewish life.

Harriet Horwitz
President, B'nai B'rith Women
1990–1992

Joan Kort
President, B'nai B'rith Women
1992–1994

ACKNOWLEDGEMENTS

I am grateful to Joan Kort, president-elect of B'nai B'rith Women, and to B'nai B'rith Women for affording me the opportunity to write this book.

I want to thank the following individuals who have answered questions and helped me in my research for this book: Rabbi Alan L. Cohen (Beth Shalom Synagogue); Rabbi Morris B. Margolies, Ph.D. (Rabbi Emeritus Beth Shalom Synagogue); Rabbi Mark H. Levin (Temple Beth Torah); Rabbi Michael Zedek (Temple B'nai Jehudah); Dr. Bill Murphy (Rolling Hills Presbyterian Church); Rev. Dick Olsen (Prairie Baptist Church); Rev. Duke Tuffy (Unitarian Church); Father Dan Murphy (Rockhurst College); Reggie Goldberg, M.S.W. (Jewish Family & Children Services); Fran Wolf (librarian, Beth Shalom Synagogue); Bev Newman (librarian, Temple B'nai Jehudah); Hilary Lewis (Central Agency for Jewish Educational Resource); Rose Evelyn Sporn, M.A. (early childhood education specialist); Ruth Esrig Brinn (author, children's books); Kelly Reichman (outreach facilitator).

I am grateful to my parents, Bee and Pro Sherman, who taught me to appreciate my Jewish heritage. My deep gratitude goes to my husband Lee, who is always there with his understanding and loving support.

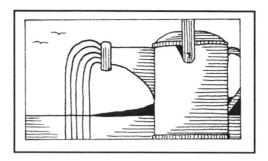

TABLE OF CONTENTS

MINGLED ROOTS
A Guide for Grandparents of Interfaith Children

TABLE OF CONTENTS (continued)

Train a child in the way he should take, and when he is old, he will not depart from it.

Proverbs: 22:6

INTRODUCTION

The Book of Proverbs was written before the age of social mobility and religious freedom. Today's children do not always follow the old ways—the ways we trained them. Change, which used to evolve over centuries, now stuns us with its rapidity. People who remember streets filled with horse-drawn vehicles have lived to see supersonic airplanes, nuclear weapons, computers, and orbiting spacecraft. Even the family, as we used to know it, has changed. Many say that the traditional Jewish family is a vanishing breed.

Today, nearly every family or extended family has experienced an interfaith marriage. Current statistics show that there are more than a *half million* Jewish/Christian couples in the United States. Of the roughly two million children under age 18 of these mixed marriages, *just over one-quarter* are being raised as Jews. Have Jewish people survived centuries of oppression only to be wiped out at the wedding altar?

Where interfaith marriages are involved, religious heritage is a delicate subject that should be approached carefully and with a healthy dose of diplomacy. Even discussing it can easily create resentment in your children and confusion in your grandchildren. Few situations are more painful than two generations at odds with one another. The parent, who has made his marital choice independent of his family's desires, quite often resents any intrusion on the part of the grandparent.

I have interviewed rabbis, priests, ministers, and scores of grandparents and interfaith couples to gain insight into what the situation looks like in the real world to those actually living it. When I started my research, it became clear that sources of information on the topic of grandparents and the non-Jewish grandchild were scarce. Books on intermarriage usually devoted only a paragraph or two to the interaction between the two generations. Consequently, I felt there was a need for a book that

book that would help family members begin to broach the often taboo subject of religious faith. Although I was told by some grandparents, "don't meddle," "don't rock the boat," "leave well enough alone," I can't leave well enough alone, not in light of present statistics. I feel grandparents have an immensely useful role to play in providing their interfaith grandchildren with knowledge about their traditions and their family heritage.

This book is not about religion *per se*. The various branches of Judaism—or even the lack of religious affiliation—are irrelevant to the matter at hand. This book is about a proud Jewish heritage, and how grandparents can do their earnest best to transmit that heritage under difficult circumstances. It is also about relationships—between you and your children, you and your children's spouses, you and your grandchildren.

The purpose of this book is to help you teach your grandchild in a non-proselytizing manner about your background, your tradition, your way of life. I, who had such loving grandparents, and who saw how much my children received from their grandparents—how could I dare do less?

This book contains specific ideas for imparting your customs and traditions to an interfaith grandchild. It offers approaches to use in making plans with the child's parents. The parents have made their religious choices. You as a grandparent need to respect that, realizing you too have choices. That you, too, have a voice. And take heart. As much as things have changed, much remains the same. Each section of this book is headed by a quotation—some dating back to biblical times—confirming that the human condition and human concerns contain constantly recurring themes.

There is an interesting adjunct to all of this as well. In your concern for imparting Jewish values to your grandchild, you will probably discover great gaps in your own knowledge. You will find yourself quite literally staggered and amazed by the wealth of beautiful material you had no idea even existed. Luckily, you have ample time—children only grow one day at a time. As you teach you will also learn. Not a bad bonus! One other brief comment. In writing this book, I have most often used "he" and "him" instead of "she" and "her" for the sake of simplicity.

When people ask me for whom did I write this book? I answer, "It is for any Jewish grandparent who wants to share the beauty and joy of his Jewish heritage: for the grandparent who wants to be remembered by his grandchild."

You are reading this book because you care. What a wonderful way to begin.

Sunie Levin

PART I
LET'S TALK

NEW BREED OF GRANDPARENT

Ten-year-old Rachel gazed at her grandmother with a quizzical look on her pert, eager face. "How come you aren't like the storybook grandmas?" she asked with a child's total sincerity. "You don't stay around the house baking strudel and cooking matzoh ball soup or sitting in your rocking chair talking. You're out playing tennis or exercising every day and it seems that every month or two you're on a jet plane flying off somewhere. Grandpa is always playing golf or gin rummy." And, she continues accusingly, "you don't let me call you Granny, or Nana, or *Bubbie* like the ones in the books. You make me call you Janet and Grandpa makes me call him Bob."

"Well," Janet said, "I'm just not that kind of grandmother, and I'm not going to change, so I guess we'll just have to change the storybooks!"

Yes, it's true. Grandparents aren't what they used to be. They are in the prime of life, and that prime is far longer than it was in Plato's time. Men and women today will find themselves in their prime at an age when most in Plato's day were long in their graves.

The traditional old-fashioned grandparent who liked to be called *Bubbie* or *Zayde* has become as rare as buffalo. Many don't like being *called* grandparents in our society that adores the young, but, all the same, they enjoy the role. And they are eager to love their grandchildren and to pass their wisdom down to them.

However, along with increased life span, there are other huge differences between now and yesteryear. The traditional grandparent was usually close by, often in the same house or at least in the same city, giving advice and emotional support as well as handing down Jewish values. With the mobility of today's families and the distance and differences in lifestyles, grandparents and grandchildren often do not have close relationships. This is especially true when hundreds or thousands of miles of separation mean that they see each other only once a year, if they're lucky. In addition, divorce, blended families, and interfaith marriage have introduced new and complex problems into the family structure.

Although grandparents may come in a new package and may live miles away, they still are the guardians of the family heritage and the nurturers of religious faith and values. As such, they have a special opportunity to build relationships that will help strengthen the Jewish heritage of their grandchildren.

There are more than 50 million grandparents in the United States today. That's a powerful group with the ability to exert tremendous influence over today's children. Until recently, grandparenthood signaled an ending stage of life. Now, we typically have almost half our lives left to live. We're vigorous, we're active, we're involved, and we have a lot to offer. The key is in finding the intelligent, effective, and loving way to do it.

Parents once taught their children to talk; today children teach their parents to be quiet.
Talmud: Sotah 49a

GRANDPARENT DIPLOMACY

What? The Talmud says that? You mean today's generation isn't the first to be rebellious? I guess not. But right this moment, at the dawning of the 21st century, the problems of Talmudic times look like a piece of cake.

As grandparents, you want and need to tell your grandchild "who we are," and you have a right to do so. It's the *how* of doing it that's so important and so difficult. In the real world you must be sensitive to the feelings of your non-Jewish son/daughter-in-law. You want, after all, to maintain the affection of your children as well as your grandchildren. Of course, that's true even in a single-faith marriage. However, with interfaith situations, you have a bomb with a short fuse that can be touched off with what often seems to be no provocation. Remember, whether or not your son- or daughter-in-law has a justifiable reason for acting resentful, he or she does have the upper hand and can deprive you of seeing your grandchildren.

It is possible you reacted strongly and did your level best to discourage the interfaith marriage from ever taking place. This may be ancient history, but it's not about to be forgotten. The time to try to mend fences is before your grandchildren are born. But, if you're reading this book, that's probably no longer an option. This book presupposes that you have made peace with the fact of the marriage. That, of course, is your personal decision. But if you haven't, put this book down immediately and plan to give it to someone else.

We must always remember that grandchildren are not our children. We're not their parents. We're not bringing them up. We don't have the responsibilities, which means we don't have the authority either. It is important for you to respect your adult children's prerogative in raising their own children. Communicate with your children. Ask them how they feel you might improve your relationship with them. Offer to babysit the grandchildren for a weekend. Breathes there the mother with hostility so deep she won't let grandma be a free babysitter?

One of the most difficult things about grandparenting is learning to use diplomacy and tact. Perhaps you didn't have the relationship you would have liked while your own children were growing up. Nature has given you a second chance. Don't blow it!

You absolutely have the right—the obligation—to speak your thoughts. But think carefully before you speak and act. Much of the time, *what* you do isn't nearly as important as *how* you do it.

This lot is bitterest, to recognize the good but by necessity to be barred from it.

Pindar (Greek poet)

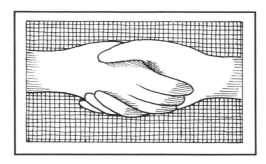

WORKING AGREEMENT

We often know what we seek to accomplish, but aren't sure how to go about it. You want to share your Jewish heritage and values with your grandchildren without offending your non-Jewish son- or daughter-in-law and without creating or exacerbating problems for your child. What to do?

First, never forget that the parent's choice of a religious identity is a private affair in keeping with his or her personal needs. It is essential that the non-Jewish spouse understands you are not competing in regard to the religious instruction of the child. Though you may not agree with the choice, acceptance and respect for that choice will make your relationship with your children and grandchildren a more harmonious one. On top of that, you scarcely have an option.

Parents may choose to raise the children in the faith of only one of the parents, Jewish or non-Jewish. They may celebrate both religions, adopt no religious belief, or let the child choose his own religious affiliation at a later date. Even if they have not yet made a decision because they can't or won't deal with the issue, that in itself is a choice—their choice. Whatever the choice, it has been made. You are dealing with an accomplished fact. You can't change it. You don't get a vote.

As a grandparent you would like to share your heritage with your grandchild. But the first rule in attempting to transmit a feeling for their heritage to your grandchildren is: *get permission from their parents. Play by their rules and be sensitive to their feelings.* Have the tact to back off if you sense resistance; tomorrow is another day. With luck, and tact, time may mellow things. Continue to develop warm, loving, non-censuring communication with your children. Let them know that, while your needs regarding family heritage are valid, you accept and respect their way of doing things in *their* home.

If you feel it would be appropriate, offer a written outline of what you specifically propose. Actually negotiate a preliminary understanding with the parents, and write it down for approval. This might seem like an off-the-wall suggestion, but in some situations it might make sense.

Your plan projected over several months could include talking to your grandchildren about who you are, and relating memories of your parents and grandparents, where they were born and what their life was like. The second month could be spent in sharing the joy of the Sabbath with a grandchild. The next month could include a visit to a temple or synagogue. The following months could be spent in holiday fun celebration and preparations, visiting a Jewish exhibit, finding Jewish books in your local book store, and going to a Jewish concert or movie at the Jewish Community Center. Try to cover everything you might like to share. Give the parents a list of the books you would like to give your grandchildren. And be sure to continually reinforce to the parents that you will adhere to what *they* feel comfortable with when you are telling their children about Judaism. The written outline may seem extreme, but it will let the parents know you are sensitive to their feelings and will allow them to hold you to your word if you try to push beyond the boundaries you've agreed to. It should give them a much higher comfort level, which makes things easier all around.

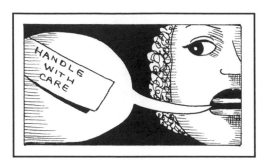

WHAT TO SAY AND HOW TO SAY IT

When asking the parents' permission to talk to your grandchild you might say, "I would like to tell Karen about me and my family roots. We may have different religions but I love you and I love my grandchild. I will not try to compete with your religious views or what you are teaching Karen. Sooner or later, everyone wants to know about his or her heritage. I'm a living link to Karen's family history."

To your non-Jewish son or daughter-in-law you might add, "I want her to know all about me, and your parents probably feel the same way about your family heritage. Our family traditions and shared identity bind us together and define who we are as a family. And we are a family. All of us."

Ask the parents for guidelines on what is acceptable and reassure them that they make the ground rules. Most importantly, make certain the non-Jewish parent knows that you will not attempt to proselytize. Your entire goal and purpose is to give the child a better sense of who he is, where he comes from, what his roots are. Make it completely clear that you are not trying to "convert" the child. And mean it. Serious problems in family relations are created by grandparents trying to convince grandchildren to accept their religion.

Keep in mind that timing is everything. You don't have to bring "Jewish" into every family gathering. Be natural and bring things up when it makes sense in the context of the situation. You can be informative, witty, thoughtful, and interesting. You can be a nuisance, an irritant, and a bore. Take your pick.

PART II
FAMILY

This sense of identity provides the ability to experience one's self as something that has continuity and sameness, and to act accordingly.

Erik Erikson, 1902

WHO AM I?

Who am I? A very good question. Children start grappling with it almost from the time they can talk. Religion gives people one answer. It provides a common history, values, traditions, rituals, stories, jokes, and more. This shared system gives them a feeling they belong to a group. What's the difference between religious identity and religious faith? Faith is what you believe; identity is where you belong. For many, the religion of their childhood gives them a sense of community. It is the place where they belong; they remain within that religion, not necessarily because they believe its particular dogmas, but because they feel comfortable there.

The preschool child wants to be like mommy or daddy. Identity and self-image are formed by taking cues from parents. They are the role models, and the child imitates what he sees and hears. He has a natural curiosity about who he is and where he belongs, and accepts what his parents tell him. As you get to know your grandchild, he will ask you questions about religious and ethnic background, and will accept your answers, too. Make certain that the parents are aware of, and comfortable with, the kind of answers you will be giving their children.

When the child is at your house, suggest making a book called "Special Me." On the cover put the child's photograph, and inside there can be separate pages that would include name, birthdate, nickname, city and state where he now lives, weight, height, and other distinguishing characteristics about hair color, eyes, and who he looks like. The book grows as he grows. He'll keep it all his life.

To really get to know your grandchild, the book "Special Me" can give you information about what he likes to eat, TV shows he watches, what interests him, and special friends he likes to play with. Whenever you're together you can ask him questions and put in new pictures along with the text. It won't be long before he'll be writing the text himself. This information will help you build a close relationship with your grandchild; he will realize that you are really interested in him and his world. Then you'll have a lot to talk about on the telephone or in letters as you begin to share with him stories about his Jewish roots.

The search for identity continues and becomes more intense during the teenage years. Children are very concerned with "who's like us" and "who's different." During junior high, peer relationships become important, and children need to figure out more precisely where they belong. During late adolescence, high school, and college, the young adult wants to know, in an entirely different sense, "Who am I?" Part of defining oneself at this stage of life is separating from parents.. It is a time of searching, of reading, of making choices. Grandparents can be there to listen and to be spiritual mentors.

It is very important for you to be knowledgeable so you can answer your grandchild's questions intelligently, thoughtfully, and accurately. There are many good books (see appendix), as well as magazines, such as *Moment* and *Commentary* that can keep you well informed.

The root of the kingdom is the state. The root of the state is the family. The root of the family is the person at its head.

Mencius (Chinese philosopher), 372-289 B.C.E.

OUR FAMILY

A preschool child knows that his family starts with his mommy and daddy and siblings. He must be taught about grandparents, aunts, uncles, and other extended family members. At this stage the child's thinking is quite concrete, so use pictures to develop the concept of extended family. Tell him that a family is people who love one another, help, share, take care of each other, and celebrate happy times together. Once the child is old enough, you might add that a Jewish family, like all families, has a certain way of thinking and has special customs or ways of doing things.

If you have a picture album, share it with your grandchild so he can see you and his parent, especially when the parent was his age or younger. Children like as much certainty as they can get in a world that is ever-new and puzzling. As they do with favorite books, they'll come back again and again to the picture album—with the same delight as when they first laid eyes on it.

Help the child make a family picture album of his own. Put a family group photo on the cover and put each family member on a separate page. You can tell your grandchild what makes each member special or interesting, how they are related to him, and then write a short summary under each picture. Put pages in a loose-leaf notebook so more can easily be added. A family tree will also help your grandchild grasp the idea of the family as a whole and how the individuals within are related.

To help your grandchildren see the familial relationships, construct a family gallery. This project is more revealing than the usual genealogical family tree since it will help you and your grandchild spot physical characteristics that distinguish your family.

When the Cohen family, for example, welcomed a new granddaughter into the family, there was no doubt that she belonged. She possessed the same unique genetic characteristic that many family members had before her—a small dimple in her chin.

At the base of the gallery put *your* parents. You go on the next level, then your children and their spouses. Point out to the grandchildren that their parents' brothers and sisters are the children's aunts and uncles. At the top rung of the gallery of photos, put your grandchildren. If they're available, you can go even further with pictures of your grandparents and, if possible, great-grandparents. You're probably going to need a *big* sheet of poster-board—it's incredible how quickly the branches spread. With photographs of the whole *mishpocha*, it's inevitable that family resemblances will come out. You'll get a kick out of it too—you'll pick up on similarities you never noticed before.

Your grandchild will have a lot of fun deciding whose red hair he inherited, whose dimples, nose, or mouth. As your grandchild grows older, if there is sufficient interest you can expand your genealogical research back several generations.

There are a number of good books, as well as archives, that you can contact for help in your quest for "roots." The *Guide Book To Jewish Genealogy* will help you get started.

HELLO, I'M YOUR GRANDPARENT

While we'd like to believe that absence does indeed make the heart grow fonder, "out of sight, out of mind" is closer to the truth. Whether you live in the same town or thousands of miles away, in order to build a close relationship with your grandchild that child needs to get to know you. He needs to spend time with you, either in person when that's possible, or via letters, pictures, and tapes when distance separates you.

Have *fun* while you are getting to know one another and the grandchild won't forget you. Start a memory drawer or trunk that contains various objects from your past. Include pictures, perhaps a Purim *gragger* (noisemaker) or Chanukah *dreidel* (top) you played with, even old clothes that you used to wear. They all have a story. Let your grandchild choose a new object for each visit and then you can tell the story. Only allow him to pick one item per visit. The old Scheherazade ploy will bring him back again and again.

Tell your grandchild that you are Jewish and would like to tell the story about where you came from and what it was like when you were young. You'll have a captive audience—the very best kind! Give as much Jewish flavor to the stories as you can. "I remember when I was about your age, I went to my grandparents' synagogue on *Simchas Torah* and I marched around carrying a flag pole with an apple stuck on top and a burning candle in the apple. We had a lot of fun!"

Tried and true openers include: "I remember...." "Let me tell you about the time...." "There was the time your mom/dad and I went to see...." Your grandchild will find each story fascinating and wait eagerly for the next one. Remember the child's age and don't make the story too long.

For your distant grandchild you'll have to introduce yourself through letters.

Share yourself, your memories, dreams, and hopes. Send along a scrapbook that can hold grandma's letters. Your letters will be read over and over again before they find their way into the scrapbook. At this age the parent, of course, will have to do the reading, but in later years they will be a treasure for the child to retain as part of his lifelong memory of you. Letter stories give grandchildren a clearer picture of their grandparents and what they believe in. The very fact that you write is important in and of itself. It shows you care enough to take the time. Everyone loves getting personal letters—especially kids.

You might want to consider taping some of the letter stories. At the same time, there are grandparent books you can buy and fill in with priceless information about your own genealogy, your parents, your thoughts, even things your own children never heard about. These books are published with the title *Grandpa* or *Grandma Remembers,* or something similar. Your child will read this book to your grandchild just as soon as it is presented, and with equal if not greater interest. It's sure to become a family heirloom.

Religion is the vision of something which stands beyond, behind and within the passing flux of immediate things.

Alfred North Whitehead, 1867-1947

WHAT'S JEWISH?

You've told your preschool grandchild that you are Jewish, but he will likely say, "What's Jewish?" Good question! Now's the time for deft answers. Keep in mind that everything you say may be micro-analyzed by your son or daughter's non-Jewish spouse. You have made a bargain not to proselytize and you must keep it.

At this age a child operates at a concrete level, hence you may need to use pictures or actual symbols to get across some of the things that explain "what's Jewish." Show and tell is the way to teach. The child will be interested in learning about new things that can be seen and touched. Handle with care. Where the concepts are specifically religious, as opposed to cultural, get the parents' approval first. If this causes discomfort, back off and stick to more generic items. Each month, as new holidays come up, stories and songs will add to the knowledge of "what's Jewish."

After age five you can introduce abstract concepts of Judaism: Jewish people believe in one God, they love learning and studying, and they try to do good deeds. You might add that Jewish people have been doing these things for a long, long time. For thousands of years Hebrew has been our language. You can show the child Hebrew writing; he'll giggle when you tell him it reads from right to left. We celebrate special holidays, say certain prayers, and have unique customs or ways of doing things. The place we go to pray is called a synagogue or temple. Jewish people feel that they are like one big family with Jews who live all over the world. This is not the whole story, of course, but at this age, it's a good beginning.

For the teenager you can explain that Jewish morality and law is the result of over 5,000 years of continuous development, and that traditional Judaism is based on revelation, custom, and ritual in both the written and oral Torah. When your grandchild's questions indicate interest, be sure to give him some of the many good books about Judaism, or attend a class or lecture together.

16

Then more than one in a thousand in the days that are yet to come, shall have some hope of the morrow, some joy of the ancient home.

William Morris, 1834-1896

JEWISH HOME BEAUTIFUL

The home. Its joys. No matter how ambivalent the feelings, for nearly everyone home is special and retains its pull.

Your grandchild comes to visit. What better place to begin his Jewish education than in your home? Hopefully, your home will have some Jewish objects and pictures. Be enthusiastic and show your enjoyment at having them about you. Tell how each is used: the *Mezzuzah* identifies a Jewish home on the outside and contains a parchment with prayers; a *Seder* plate is used at Passover to display symbols of the holiday.

Suggest that you play a game. Tell your little detective that he can go on a treasure hunt to see how many Jewish objects he can find in your home. You might want to supply a list. If you don't have the object, hide its picture in a not-too-difficult-to-find place. After he finds everything on the list, the child can draw pictures of the objects and write or dictate a story to go with each picture. Have a special prize like a coloring book on hand when he finishes.

An older child will enjoy inspecting the Sabbath candlesticks that your great-grandmother brought to America and will like hearing an explanation of the *Ketubah* (marriage contract) that you have hanging on your wall. Whatever age your grandchildren are, you can share "who I am" along with your home and way of life.

But what if you are more secular and your home isn't filled with Jewish symbols? Or what if, in "taking the temperature" of your relationship with your son-in-law or daughter-in-law you sense that this activity might be perceived as too intrusive or a breach of the contract you negotiated? You still have room to maneuver. You can rearrange your home so that the objects are more highly visible, and can find pictures or buy objects that, for you, represent the proper Jewish cultural relevance. If the child asks about these things, you surely have every right to answer and explain.

LIVING ANCESTORS, AND OTHERS

Add the tales you have heard from your parents and grandparents to those growing out of your own experiences, and you soon realize that *you* provide a long and important link to the past for your children and grandchildren. Most of us, typically, can transmit an oral history that spans as much as 125 years.

School-age children begin to learn they have a past through their parents' reminiscences. All of a sudden it dawns on them that they have living ancestors in their grandparents. Grandma and Grandpa provide a sense that the family was here before and will continue to thrive. "Grandpa, tell me that weird story about how it was before TV and computers." Grandpa's story gives the child roots and makes him feel secure. (He may also find it awesome that times could ever have been so primitive!)

Share the proud particulars about your Jewish heritage; you'll never have a more eager audience. Children love to hear the details. My own grandfather sang on the Yiddish stage in New York. My grandkids love to hear me tell them stories about it.

If yours are long-distance grandchildren, tell them the stories on tape, either audio or video.

Storytelling, or sharing life memories with others, is a valuable form of communication, not just for your heirs, but for yourself as well. Your story is your unique contribution. Telling about your life experiences often helps you tie-up some unfinished business and allows you to review your life and put things in perspective.

By the time a child is 10, he may develop an interest in genealogy. That's the time to begin a joint research project with him. It will give you hours of shared experiences that undoubtedly will draw you much more closely together. What's more, it will be a superb opportunity to dwell at length on the Jewish branch of the family tree. Almost every family has them—stories of ancestors before they came to America, or what it was like to be Jewish in Poland, Lithuania, Russia, or wherever the family is from. Such stories are fascinating and offer food for dozens of hours of discussion. On top of that, you'll probably get hooked on the project yourself. During your research, you may find yourself discovering relatives you never knew you had and details of family history that may come as a surprise—or even an embarrassment!

Laws are sand, customs are rock. Laws can be evaded and punishment escaped, but an openly transgressed custom brings sure punishment.

Mark Twain, 1835-1910

FAMILY RITUALS TELL US WHO WE ARE

Family rituals bind us together and tell us who we are as a family. Some moments are quickly forgotten; others will be savored for decades and passed on to future generations. With the help of parents' reminiscences, children come to understand that they have a past. Be it a holiday festival or a family's passion for certain recipes, the ritual bridges the generations and establishes a collective identity.

Rituals define our family relationships. Some are religiously oriented, like finding the hidden *afikomen* at Passover or lighting the Chanukah candles. Others are purely secular, but unique to the family. Whatever the activity, the parents and children consider it an important part of their identity as a family. A sense of "we-ness" grows out of a shared ritual and strengthens family closeness. This is especially important when combining traditions from two families.

Learn to respect the rituals your adult children celebrate in their own homes, even if they are not the ones you are accustomed to. This can involve a major adjustment on your part. Unfamiliar rituals may seem silly, bizarre, or outlandish. On the other hand, think for a moment how the festive party that goes with a *bris* (ritual circumcision) must look to a non-Jew, and it might give you a better perspective. Even with a marriage of spouses of the same faith, there are differences. Did you dip your finger into the glass or pour wine into a saucer as the plagues were read at Passover? Which grandfather did it which way? Why? It made for lively discussion at our Passover each year.

Of course you'll want to tell your grandchildren about the rituals their mother or father enjoyed with you when they were growing up. You can even make a ritual out of the telling. A grandmother giving her granddaughter an old family recipe is giving more than a cooking lesson; the message received is something special and is part of her heritage.

When asked about happy memories from childhood, most times they involve rituals—eating the same food, singing the same songs, saying a prayer. Rituals have a sense of permanence and certainty, and in the world today, children need to feel that some things won't change. Traditional holidays that the family enjoys together are certainly remembered. But each time you see your grandchildren you can make a deposit in their memory bank. At our house, when the grandkids ring the doorbell, Grandpa always lowers his voice an octave and says menacingly, "Who's...that...ringing...my...doorbell!" It's silly, but the kids always laugh, and they'll probably always remember.

REUNIONS

Family reunions. This is the time to let your grandkids see what family is all about, *if* you've got the nerve! Hopefully, you have gotten smart since the last one, the one where *you* did all the work and had to listen to all the other relatives complain. This time, plan it away from your house. Meet at a place that is centrally located and where the kids will have plenty to do. Then delegate. Give everyone a job. Consider assigning committees. Have a housing and food director, a director for social events, and a program planner. Actually half the fun is in the planning. Let the kids be in on it. Plan games and activities according to age groups. Ask everyone to bring photos and write reminiscences of past events. The idea is to share family togetherness.

As a natural part of the process, your grandchildren are going to learn about all the relationships that link these people; with the living faces right before their eyes.

Be sure to have a video camera, tape recorder, or even a professional photographer for the family picture. And keep in mind that even if the reunion turns out to be a disaster, it will be a source of remembered hilarity for years to come. And you'll have it all documented on videotape, else no one would ever believe it!

During the program, your grandchildren will hear all the *bubbemeises* (old wives' tales), and a skeleton or two might wind up being dragged out of the family closet. If *that* doesn't give them a feel for their roots, it's hard to imagine what else will!

FAMILY NEWSLETTER

The key to relationships is communication. This holds true for a relationship across many miles, as well as under the same roof. As grandparents, we must keep the lines of communication open. So, instead of waiting beside the telephone or searching the contents of the mailbox, initiate something—a family newsletter.

Get that old typewriter down off the shelf, dust if off, and get started. Of course, nowadays, chances are you have a desk-top computer and maybe a fax machine as well! Anyhow, here's a true story:

Grandpa Meyer, way out in Parsons, Kansas, edits and publishes his own newspaper, a simple photocopy job. His grandchildren are his "foreign correspondents." He loves to clip cartoons from magazines and tape them to the master copy (they photocopy well). He gets the entire family all over the country into the act. Even the youngest children send their latest drawings. His family newsletter is called "Meyer's Talk," and it comes out monthly. He covers a myriad of topics, but always includes the holiday being celebrated that month—what the different family members are doing for it, a story about the holiday (everybody suspects he simply makes most of them up), some songs, jokes, and a few pointed political barbs. Meyer makes sure he gives some advice and usually has fun roasting a member of the family.

The newsletter started out at one page and has grown to four because all the family members want to contribute. It has become the vehicle that has drawn the family closer together despite the distances that separate them. Is he passing down family heritage? You bet! Will his great-grandchildren remember him? For sure. Will his newsletters be saved and treasured and read by future generations? Of course! In fact, most of the family members have put the newsletters into a three-ring binder for family history. Meyer has made certain that he is one member of the family who simply will not be forgotten.

And now for the punch line. Meyer is almost 90 years old. If Meyer can do it, you can too.

PART III
CUSTOMS &
TRADITIONS

Wait for the wisest of all counselors. Time.

Pericles, 495-429 B.C.E.

TRADITION

What is tradition? Is it simply Tevye singing and telling his daughter whom she should marry?   Joseph B. Soloveitchik, a leading rabbinic scholar, notes three traditions that have historically run through Judaism, all being intrinsic to the basic faith. The first tradition is Torah, which he relates to intellect, reason, and knowledge. Next is that of *mitzvot*, of doing and observing. Third is that of *regesh*, of feeling, of emotion, and sentiment. Will your grandchild experience the emotions you do when you hear "Hatikvah," Israel's national anthem? Have you told him about the goose bumps you have when you hear the *shofar* blown on Yom Kippur or how you get tears of pride in your eyes when your youngest grandchild recites the Four Questions on Passover?

Take your grandchild to an Israel Independence Day celebration so he can feel the spirit and pride of the Jewish people. Whether a traditional or secular Jew, we all feel a void in our lives if we are raised without a clear sense of our heritage. A Jewish life, reflecting the authentic values and lifestyle of the Jewish heritage in all its beauty, can give added meaning to your grandchild's life.

To a large extent, tradition is the principal thing you can hope to impart to your grandchild. In one way or another, just about everything in this book has to do with the passing down of Jewish traditions in the hope of keeping them alive. And the very best part of the endeavor is this. There is no way you can possibly lose. Any measure of success is more than would have been attained had you simply not tried at all.

MY VERY OWN JEWISH CALENDAR

You help your grandchild celebrate a birthday; now he can help you celebrate some of the Jewish holidays. He will need a calendar so he can tell when each one is coming. Keeping track of Jewish holidays can be tricky for a youngster, considering the way they seem to skip around the calendar from year to year.

A Hebrew calendar can be purchased, or you can use the B'nai B'rith Women planning calendar. But it's more fun to make a calendar when you are together, or send one you have made yourself. Buy a large pad of white art paper, 12" x 16", draw lines and numbers, then paste holiday picture symbols on the right day and month.

Your young grandchild can have fun coloring a holiday coloring book and then cutting out and pasting on the symbols, or you can buy Jewish holiday stickers at the local temple bookstore. As you both are cutting and pasting, the child can learn a few things about each of the holidays.

Be sure to call or send a card (either a store-bought one or one you have made), a holiday book and perhaps a holiday game when each holiday comes. This will help reinforce your grandchild's new-found knowledge so that these holidays won't be easily forgotten.

By age six a child can have the difference between the solar calendar and the lunar calendar explained to him. I'm taking it for granted that you, of course, understand the lunar calendar. If you don't, now's a great time for you and your grandchild to learn together. Today's young ones are really smart and somewhere out there there's undoubtedly a computer program that will let you know when Chanukah comes 100 years from now.

For older children, buy a copy of the *Standard Guide to the Jewish & Civil Calendar 1899-2050*. Your grandchildren will have hours of fun looking up the changes in the calendar.

An idea, in the highest sense of the word, cannot be conveyed but by a symbol.
Samuel Taylor Coleridge, 1772-1834

SYNAGOGUE VISIT

Most religions are big on symbols and Judaism is no exception. You've shared the Jewish symbols in your home with your grandchild. If his parents agree, you may want to show him the intriguing symbols in the synagogue as well.

Before your visit, explain the various objects and show pictures of what he will see: the tablets of the Ten Commandments, the *Ner Tamid* (eternal light), the *Siddur* (prayer book), the Ark, and beautiful Torahs (scrolls) inside, and real live people called the Rabbi and Cantor. A personal tour when no one else is around is best for the first time.

You'll want to explain that the synagogue is a holy place and there are rules about not talking or running about during the service. Also, explain that you stand when the holy Ark is open and when the Torah is carried around the synagogue. If possible, have someone open the Ark so the child can see the Torah up close. Explain about the mantle, breastplate and *yad* (pointer). The more familiar the child can become with the names of the new objects, the more he'll enjoy them. Reinforce the visit with a book about the synagogue and perhaps a domino game of religious objects. These are available at most Jewish gift shops. Let the child know that Jews have fun and enjoy their religion.

With a younger child be aware of his short attention span. Don't overstay the visit if the child becomes extra squirmy. Next time you might try attending a *Bar* or *Bat Mitzvah* or a *Purim* or *Simchat Torah* service, where there is plenty of action.

Again—never, never take the child to the synagogue without first discussing it with his parents.

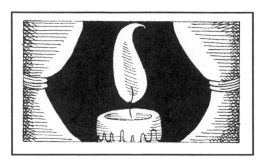

SABBATH EXPERIENCE

The Sabbath can be a day of delight and joy for you and your grandchild. If possible, invite the child to spend Friday night with you so that together you can welcome the Sabbath. In your explanation tell the child that the Ten Commandments tell us to "Remember the Sabbath day to keep it holy." Read the story of Creation to the child, telling how God worked to create the world for six days and on the seventh day, He rested. That day we call Sabbath, a special day of rest, prayer, and fun with the family. Although your grandchild may celebrate Sabbath on Sunday, you can let him know that the Jewish Sabbath is Saturday.

Let your grandchild help you get ready for the Sabbath. Ask him to shine your candlesticks or silverware and set the table on the pretty white cloth. Tell him to change into good clothes for Sabbath dinner. Helping you prepare the food can be fun, especially baking a challah together. There is nothing more satisfying to a child of any age than to break eggs into a bowl, mix the ingredients, and knead the dough on a board. It's exciting to watch the dough double in size, to pound it down, and braid it for challah. And the aroma while it's baking—can't you smell it?

Oh, you buy yours at the delicatessen? Well, take the child with you. Delicatessens smell great, too.

As you welcome the Sabbath by lighting the candles let the child watch you and join in saying *Shabbat Shalom* to everyone. Teach him the other blessings so he can help grandpa say the *Kiddush* and the *hamotzi* over the challah.

And after you all enjoy the wonderful meal that your grandchild has helped you make, sing songs together. Let him feel the joy and peace of the Sabbath. If you truly savor the Sabbath, the child will know it, and remember.

LEARNING A NEW VOCABULARY

Children love to add new words to their vocabularies. They pick them up quickly, especially the ones you don't want them to know! Part of learning about you and your Jewish heritage is discovering new words. They'll need simple explanations for the abstract words like kosher, and for the Hebrew blessings you say at the Sabbath table. The concrete words they'll learn quickly, especially if they have a picture or symbol for *shofar, menorah,* and *seder* plate. Games like picture lotto can help them match pictures with words and, at the same time, teach them how to pronounce and define the object. Synagogue and Jewish community center gift shops have excellent games and books you can use.

Children enjoy learning new and different words, particularly at ages five through seven. Hebrew words and phrases will get their attention, and usually a giggle. Don't forget to let them know that portions of the Bible were written in Hebrew, and that it is spoken in Israel. You can explain that a boy or girl who has a *bar* or *bat mitzvah* must learn a portion of the Torah in Hebrew. Some of the common words and phrases you might like to teach include:

Shalom	hello and goodbye
Morah	teacher
Todah	thank you
Shabbat Shalom	have a happy sabbath
Boker tov	good morning
Layelah tov	good night
Mazel tov	need I translate?

Doubtless you will have your own words and phrases—some Hebrew, some Yiddish, some who knows? For the most part, there really won't be any need to "teach" them. If you just *say* the words when it's appropriate, they'll pick them up. Because you adore your grandchildren, and they know it, they will try to please you by using some of the words when they are with you.

ANOTHER NEW LANGUAGE: YINGLISH

Spanish is fun and Pig Latin is great, but wait until your grandchild tries some of the Yiddish expressions that have become Americanized. Let the child know that although Hebrew is the "official" language of the Jewish people, Yiddish came about when the Jews were spread all over the world. It combines some German, Polish, and Russian with Hebrew to form its own unique flavor and sound. Yiddish developed out of necessity because Hebrew words didn't always provide what was needed to buy groceries, for example, or ask for directions. Further, Hebrew was regarded as the holy language for praying and studying the Bible, and so an everyday language was needed for cooking, flirting, selling or yelling at the kids. I'm sure you remember your parents or grandparents speaking Yiddish when they wanted to say things they didn't want the kids to understand.

Oy vay, tushy, and *schlep* need no interpretation. They have passed into the English language and are used by Jew and non-Jew alike, along with many other Yiddish words and phrases. *Kibbitz* and *mazel tov* have found their way into *Webster's*. Your grandchild may have already picked up on these words. Why not? *Everyone* uses them. But it wouldn't hurt to look them up in the dictionary and show they're derived from Yiddish. Here's a brief sample with definitions in case one or two might have drifted out of your memory:

kibbitz	to make comments when not asked
goniff	a thief
schlemiel	a foolish person
schmaltz	melted fat; also, very sentimental
schlep	to drag along
chutzpah	nervy
nudnik	a nuisance

Some sayings in Yiddish include *gezunterheit* (when someone sneezes, wishing them good health). Webster gives *Gesundheit* and credits only German; we put another syllable in, giving it more *schmaltz*! *Kine-ahora* is an expression said to ward off the evil eye when things are going well. And if you succeed in introducing this bit of *schmaltz* into your grandchild's vocabulary, *mazel tov!*

Heaven holds a place for those who pray...

Paul Simon (Mrs. Robinson), b. 1942

HOW DO WE PRAY?

We live in an age when praying is unfashionable. In some circles, it's almost considered embarrassing.

Yet, when one feels lonely or anxious or, perhaps, elated, the words seem to appear. Dear God, please make my brother Sam well and I'll double my contribution to B'nai B'rith Women. Thank God, we didn't get on that plane that crashed yesterday. Lord, I've never seen such a beautiful grandbaby.

Many people do not know how to pray; they are never properly taught. Seeing a grandparent pray can be quite comforting to a child. Even when the parent doesn't have the child say any prayers, by observing you, the message comes through: if grandma and grandpa pray, it must be good. Tell your grandchild that you pray when you want to talk to God; that people can make up their own prayers; they don't always have to be in a prayer book.

Explain that Jewish families say prayers together at the synagogue or temple. The Hebrew prayer book, the *siddur*, has many different kinds of prayers: Prayers when we are in need and afraid, and prayers to God giving thanks for the good things in our lives. Jewish law says it is our duty and privilege to pray.

Accompanying a grandparent to a Friday night service can be a special treat. The grandchild will feel grown-up and important in his good clothes, and he'll get to stay up past his bedtime, which most youngsters love. If the child is old enough to understand, explain some of the prayers and songs in the service. It will make the experience more interesting and meaningful. A service especially geared to young families with children is usually shorter and will give the child the opportunity to see how parents, grandparents, and children can pray together. If the child is old enough you could explain that observant Jewish men put on *tefillin* (phylacteries) on the forehead and arm. These are little boxes that contain parchments with biblical passages to remind the person of their Jewish faith. You might show the child pictures of a person wearing a *tefillin*. For religious Jews this is one of the duties connected with the morning prayers. Of course, most American Jews are not Orthodox.

Older grandchildren can be told that learning the *Shema* and *Shemoneh Esreh* prayers is both a mitzvot and an obligation as a Jew. *A Parent's Guide to Teaching Children Mitzvot* (see appendix) gives a comprehensive explanation of the benefit of prayer in our life.

Watching families at prayer can be a very satisfying and comforting experience. Your grandchild is under constant pressure today to excel, to be number one. Peer pressures, emotional stresses of divorce in the family, or dad's lost job can also take a tremendous toll. Learning the value of prayer at an early age can help fortify your grandchild spiritually for the tribulations he will encounter throughout life.

The place where services are held is not called a sanctuary by accident. Your grandchild should know that such a place exists, and that he is welcome there.

He capers, he dances, he has eyes of youth, he writes verses, he speaks holiday, he smells April and May.
William Shakespeare, 1564-1616

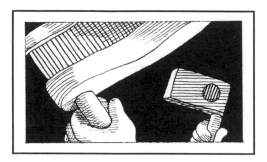

HOLIDAY FUN

If you are fortunate enough to have grandchildren close by at holiday time you'll be able to build some special memories. Let your grandchild know that holidays are holy days but also they are happy days, particularly when the family can be together to celebrate. In fact, most times it's having the family together that gives the holiday its special meaning.

Holidays like Passover, Sukkot, and Chanukah are a good time *to invite the other grandparents, if it is agreeable.* In all likelihood, the other grandparents will find these occasions to be of great interest. You'll probably be asked questions you can't answer, but that's O.K. Even rabbis have that problem from time to time.

Tell your grandchild that celebrating each Jewish holiday is an important part of being Jewish. In this context, it is perfectly appropriate to explain everything you can about the particular holiday: its origin, its significance, the meaning of the rituals and symbols, even the stories about family customs and the way things were done by your own parents and grandparents. As you enjoy the traditions together, you'll pass them down as a treasure for future generations.

Your grandchild will enjoy having a special holiday scrapbook where photographs of holiday parties, recipes, games, and stories can be included. The scrapbook could have the title *Holiday Fun*. If you want a celebration to stand out in the child's memory, add the recipe for a special food that the child helped cook plus the results of a craft project, like a matzoh cover, that can be kept and used again. See the appendix for a number of story and craft books that are appropriate for the holidays.

Make the most of holiday celebrations, especially if you're able to have your grandchildren participate. Holidays not only make great memories, their celebration lets your grandchild know he is part of a rich heritage.

Man eats to live, he does not live to eat.

Abraham ibn Ezra, 1055-1135

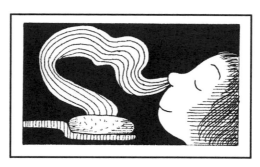

WHAT'S JEWISH COOKING?

Chicken soup! Can't you smell it cooking in your grandmother's kitchen? Often called "Jewish penicillin," everyone knows it can cure a head cold, or whatever else ails you. Its curative powers are legendary, even outside the Jewish community.

Each family has its own special recipe for matzoh balls. Some are so dense, if dropped from an airplane, they would sink a battleship; others so fluffy they need an anchor to stay in the soup. A frequent comment is "no one can make them like grandma."

Many children are already familiar with bagels and chopped liver, but now is the time to expand their knowledge of Jewish cooking. If you want a holiday that your grandchild will fondly remember, be sure to include cooking or baking some traditional foods among the activities. The child can help prepare many of the dishes.

Carry on a light conversation about the holiday while baking and preparing food. You are helping the child remember some of the holiday words and traditions. It's always a nice touch to give the child a copy of the recipe to take home. Nearly every traditional food will have its own story; as you cook, explain why Jews eat potato *latkes* for Chanukah, *charoses* for Passover, and *hamantashen* for Purim. You get the idea.

If the child is a distance away, send a care package. Remember the packages when you were in college? What child doesn't love getting baked goods from Grandma? And if, perchance, Grandma doesn't do much cooking anymore, you can buy the goodies at the delicatessen or kosher butcher shop and send them by overnight mail.

The one who causes a good deed is as meritorious as the one who performs it.
Talmud: Sanhedrin 99b

MITZVAH

The concept of *Mitzvah* is easily understood by most children: sharing and doing good for others. They hear this frequently from their parents. It's a somewhat similar concept to *tzedakah*, but not quite. And whether or not it's presented to them using the Hebrew words or the English equivalents, it all comes out the same. It's all part of being a good person. Let your grandchildren know that being a good person is an important part of the Jewish religion; that by doing good we are doing something God has commanded us to do. Although it's a privilege, it's our duty too.

The child will be amazed when he hears there are 613 separate *mitzvot*. That's a bunch. But, fundamentally, we're talking about doing good things, right things. And all of them aren't hard to do. One of those 613 is simply to wash our hands before meals. You're not going to try to master the whole list; just try to get the concept across.

You can tell them that it's a *mitzvah* to enjoy and rest on the Sabbath and that praying and studying are *mitzvot*. Make a list of different *mitzvot* with the child. Then plan a *mitzvah* that you can do together, like visiting someone at a nursing home. Tell the child how good you feel inside when you have done a *mitzvah* for someone. They'll get the idea immediately—especially when they perform one.

Tell me the tales that to me were so dear.
Long, long ago, long, long ago.

Thomas Haynes Bayley, 1797-1839

READ ME A STORY

Whether the request is for a Bible story or a holiday tale, when you hear "read me a story, Grandma," you drop everything. Don't you love it when the child snuggles up close while you read the book? You can start reading to your grandchild as soon as he can sit still for a few minutes. There are many wonderful books to give to a grandchild of any age. Clothes are outgrown and toys destroyed, but books are put up on a shelf, kept, and re-read. Favorites are even passed down to the next generation. It's entirely possible that you still have a favorite or two that were read to you, and, if you're lucky, you'll get a special kick out of reading them to your own grandchildren.

For the preschool and school-age child, whether you are a distance away or in town, tape the book so the child can listen to your voice and enjoy the story over and over. I send a book and tape of a Jewish legend or a Bible story to my long-distance grandchildren at least once a month. Be sure to send a new book appropriate for each holiday. This will not only give you something to discuss with the child, it will also give him a background of Jewish stories.

One grandfather adapted English translations of stories by Sholom Aleichem. The essence of the stories is the joy members of a Jewish family in Eastern Europe feel as they prepare their home for Passover. Sholom Aleichem tells each of the stories from the viewpoint of a young Jewish boy as he interacts with his home environment. While the setting is 19th century Europe, the plot and characters remain universal.

Holiday stories are fun to enact after hearing them. Children love to pretend. You might encourage your grandchildren to put on a play based on a holiday tale. If they're close by, join in the fun. Long-distance "actors and actresses" can ask mother and dad to tape their performance and send you a copy.

Reading books, sending books, even enacting stories all help impart a Jewish message, but they also stimulate the child's interest in reading. College SAT scores continue to reflect a dismal trend in the general literacy of American children. By encouraging a love of reading, and setting an example, you can be immensely helpful in improving your grandchild's entire academic career—his entire life, as a matter of fact.

The direction in which education starts a man will determine his future life.

Plato, 428-348 B.C.E.

BAR AND BAT MITZVAH

One of the most impressive services that your grandchild might see is a *Bar* or *Bat Mitzvah*. Considering the interfamily links it's certainly possible that he will have occasion to go to one. Explain that the ceremony is a 'coming of age' according to Jewish law; that a child who is *Bar* or *Bat Mitzvah* is no longer treated as a minor but as an adult. Girls at age 12 and boys at age 13 are considered old enough to keep the commandments and be responsible for their own deeds and acts.

Having spent a number of years in Hebrew school, the young person becoming *Bar* or *Bat Mitzvah* is ready to assume the responsibilities of being an adult. Hopefully he will continue in his Jewish studies.

After the service, there is usually a *kiddush* and festive meal. If you take your grandchild, doubtless you will pick the synagogue or temple that makes you most comfortable. The key thing is not so much the ceremony itself, but the opportunity it gives you to concretely demonstrate the emphasis Jews have always placed on education. The sight of another child—maybe a contemporary—reading a long passage in Hebrew can't help but be impressive and, if nothing else, can help your own grandchild see that, even at a young age, with dedication and hard work, much can be accomplished.

You can tell the child that the occasion marks the taking of the first steps towards Jewish responsibility. Perhaps you can tell them stories of your own memories of some of the things that took place as their mother or father was preparing for the ceremony. It will give them a better idea of what it is all about. One of our daughters developed a severe case of hives on that day, and another went through the ceremony running a high fever. But the show must go on!

With faith there are no questions; without faith, there are no answers.

The Chofetz Chaim, 1838-1933

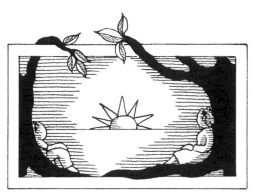

SHARE SPIRITUALITY

By talking and example, you show that your Jewish heritage and principles inspire you. Let your grandchild see that, for you, your faith is a joy and gives pleasure and meaning to your life. Let him observe you at prayer and saying the blessings on the Sabbath. If you are going to be a role model, you have to live the role.

And if your orientation is more secular, think about what it is about being Jewish that you want to transmit to your grandchild. Then make a genuine, affirmative, consistent effort to be a living example of your principles. For many, the essence of being Jewish is not found in rituals but rather in a life view; a way of involvement in the world that is unique. While you must consciously try not to undermine the value system being instilled by his parents, you can share with your grandchild those elements of life that you perceive as being special and different because of your Jewish viewpoint.

Take your grandchild on a walk and point out all the beauty in nature. Share a poem, song, or story that moves you. The child may enjoy going to an art gallery, or a Jewish community center to participate in a holiday activity. When the child asks you about God, you'll need to be able to answer how you feel and what Judaism says about God. These questions will probably lead you to do some intense soul-searching.

You may want to talk about times you have prayed to God or may have felt close to God. Share your feelings about how you are thankful for the beauty of nature that God has created and for your lovely family and friends. Share how good you feel about being Jewish and encourage the child to share his thoughts about God. Be sure to let him know that there are no "right" or "wrong" thoughts or feelings about God; that different people have different ideas about who and what God is, and that we need to respect each of those ideas.

You've already promised not to proselytize. Keep your promise.

And the jocund rebecks sound
To many a youth, and many a maid,
Dancing in the checkered shade.
And young and old come forth to play
On a sunshine holiday.

John Milton, 1608-1674

CHRISTMAS/CHANUKAH CELEBRATIONS

If you are going to try to compete with the hype of a commercial Christmas today, forget it. You'll lose hands down. The glitter and the festive atmosphere have an undeniable attraction, and even your Jewish grandchild may want to be part of the excitement. Don't worry. He won't be deprived if he doesn't get a chance to celebrate it. Rather, when Jewish grandparents try to celebrate Christmas, they deprive their grandchild of an opportunity to feel proud of his own Jewish heritage. In fact, it enormously weakens all you've been trying to accomplish.

Dr. Alice Ginott emphasizes that Jewish children should be given a positive attitude toward Chanukah. Have your non-Jewish grandchildren and your children's in-laws, as well as the parents, over for a Chanukah party. Let them see and share the warmth and positive spirit in your home. You prepare the *latkes*; let the grandchildren make the Chanukah cookies. If you have the batter ready in the refrigerator, the children can roll it out and use cookie cutters with Chanukah symbols. The baking only takes a few minutes, and it can be so satisfying for the child to find the one cookie he or she has made.

This will lead naturally to telling the Chanukah story perhaps with stick puppets the children have made. Emphasize that Chanukah was the Jewish peoples' first battle for religious freedom. When it's time, light the candles in the menorah, say the blessing and sing the songs. You might duplicate song sheets for everyone. Don't forget to have a rousing *dreidel* game; you can teach everyone how to play. You might have pennies or poker chips to play with and prizes for the winners. The message you're transmitting is, "we can *all* enjoy and share this holiday." At the same time, you are passing down symbols and traditions of your Jewish heritage.

But don't forget about equal time. If you are invited to a Christmas dinner at your children's home or the other grandparents' home, make a special effort to go. And most importantly, don't try to compete with the other grandparents at this time. This is their holiday, not yours. Keep in mind that yours is not the only cultural heritage being passed down to your grandchildren.

PART IV
VALUES &
ETHICS

Das eigentliche Studium der Menscheit ist der Mensch. *(The proper study of mankind is man.)*
Goethe, 1749-1832

TO BE A MENSCH

How do we raise a child to be good? Teach him to act like a *mensch*. So, what's a *mensch*? A *mensch* is a person who has character and dignity and a sense of what's right. A *mensch* is decent and kind and, in a world filled with pressures to look out only for number one, a *mensch* really cares about others.

The best way to teach is, of course, by example, by letting children see that their grandparent is someone to be proud of because of the way he lives and treats others. The only real way to teach your grandchild to be a *mensch* is to be one yourself. Anything else is blatant hypocrisy and children have an unerring eye for hypocrites.

The term '*mensch*' is used in many contexts. "Be a *mensch*" might be advice given to someone who is not treating another person fairly. "He's not a *mensch*" might tell you to avoid association with the person, in business or otherwise.

Can you help make a *mensch* out of your grandchild? If you're close, you may have some influence. And when you say "you're becoming quite a *mensch*," he'll know it's a major compliment.

Wealth maketh many friends.

Proverbs 19:4

HEIRLOOMS

Family treasures are passed along from generation to generation. You probably have one—a special family heirloom—in your attic or den. It might not be museum quality, but it holds enduring value to you and your family.

More often than not, heirlooms represent an intangible kind of wealth. They are priceless not for what they would bring on the open market, but rather for what they mean.

Heirlooms must start somewhere, why not with you? Make a patchwork quilt that will tell the story of your family. It will become a symbol of love and faith and always remind family members of home. Such a quilt can be made taking pieces of clothing from different family members—perhaps a *babushka* or grandma's apron. Each item in the quilt will have its own history. Record that history in a book so that the tale behind each fragment will not be lost. Your heirloom quilt and its accompanying book will be lovingly used and passed down for generations.

Making an "heirloom" with your grandchild will give it special meaning. Try a *challah* cover with stencils or embroidery, or a Sabbath tablecloth in crewel. You'll have memories as well as an heirloom to treasure.

Your family may already have heirlooms—treasures brought from Europe, for instance, when Grandma or great-Grandma's family "came over." Lucky you. Now make sure to point them out and explain them to your grandchildren. I have a crocheted tablecloth made when my grandmother's eyes were too bad to see, but her fingers still found the thread and created the pattern. It won first prize at the Nebraska state fair. My problem is going to be how to decide which of my three daughters will appreciate it most. An old *siddur* is yellowed and falling apart, but think of those whose fingers lovingly touched those pages! When you tell your story and give your heirloom to a grandchild as a prized possession, he or she will indeed come to consider it exactly that.

JEWISH HISTORY

To give your teenage grandchildren a sense of recent Jewish history, take them with you on a trip to New York and visit the Jewish Museum. If you live within driving distance, it's easy. If not, watch for low air fares; there are usually some bargains around. Hotels in New York are another matter altogether. If you have a relative in or near the city, use a little *chutzpah* and ask if you can spend a night or two; I bet the answer will be yes.

After you visit the museum, take a trip to the Lower East Side to visit a Jewish bookstore, perhaps to buy a book or a ceremonial object. Your grandchild is sure to be interested in all the exotic-looking items, as well the scores of different renditions of more familiar things—Chanukah *menorahs*, for example. There are pictures to give the child a feeling for what Delancy and Orchard Streets were like when they were teeming with people selling *knishes*, clothes, and everything else imaginable from pushcarts. Then, every store was Jewish; now all is changed—but what a time it was!

Go to Ellis Island to see the place where Jews came through immigration from Germany, Poland, and all parts of Europe. My own *zayde* left Poland with only three loaves of bread and a bottle of water for the several-week journey. At least that's the family legend—I rather suspect he had another snack or two along the way. As a poor immigrant he traveled in the bowels of the ship (they used to call it "steerage"), but he, along with many others, wept when he was able to come on deck and see the Statue of Liberty in the harbor of New York.

Where did it all begin? Before you take your trip, do a bit of research so you can relate chronologically the history of the Jews. From 1900 B.C.E. with Abraham, Sarah, Isaac, Rebekah, Jacob, Rachel, Leah, Joseph, Moses and on through the important

48

events of history, there is an unbroken narrative thread that is fascinating to Jew and non-Jew alike. Suggest your grandchild make a time line. If he or she resists, purchase one of the many charts that depict the parallel events in history. If you have the wall space, it would be great to have it mounted in your home. Most of these charts are big, so you might have to be content with opening it on the floor. And if your grandchild doesn't become absorbed in studying it, *you* probably will.

There are films (*Hester Street*, *The Chosen*, *Lies My Father Told Me*), as well as books that will give the child quite a bit to learn, as well as a feeling of continuity and permanence. The Jewish people have been around for a long time and, despite incredible struggles, have kept their identity and their traditions alive.

If you can't make the trip to New York, the bibliography in the back of this book will give you some excellent source material. Many larger cities have a museum or library with Jewish books and objects; they can serve as your resource center. It's truly never too late to learn. And in the course of sharing your Jewish values with your grandchild, you're going to find yourself learning far more than you can possibly begin to teach.

IMPORTANT PEOPLE

Whatever else your grandchildren may feel, they can be immensely proud of the Jewish blood that flows through their veins. Jews have dominated many areas of human creativity far, far in excess of their numbers. Though Jews are less than one-half of one percent of the world's population, they represent some fifteen percent of the Nobel Laureates.

Since Moses himself, Jews in every era have stood center stage and played a role in molding history. The roster of Jewish genius is incredible—Sigmund Freud and Albert Einstein; the conquerors of polio Albert Sabin and Jonas Salk; the Tin Pan Alley songsmiths George Gershwin, Jerome Kern, Irving Berlin, and Oscar Hammerstein; the Hollywood moguls Samuel Goldwyn and Louis B. Mayer. Karl Marx and Benjamin Disraeli. Yehudi Menuhin, Arthur Rubinstein, and Leonard Bernstein. This entire book could be filled with immediately recognizable names of famous Jews. Jewish genius in every realm of human achievement is legendary, and a source of immense, justifiable pride. (See appendix for books about Jewish history.)

Encourage your grandchild to read the biographies of outstanding Jews and write short stories about them.

If all men were just, there would be no need of valor.

Agesilaus, 444-400 B.C.E.

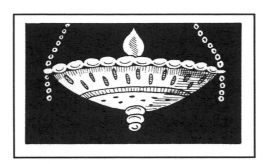

JEWISH ETHICS AND VALUES

Every day on television your grandchildren learn that sex, violence, drugs, lying, cheating, and stealing are the norm. In 1939, moviegoers were shocked to hear Clark Gable say "damn" on screen. Now, the "f-word" has crept down from "X" to "PG." In a dual-career family, parents may be too busy to teach some of the needed values. Grandparents, if it's O.K. with mom and dad, you can help.

Judaism has always seen ethics as compatible with man's ability to reason and his will to choose. We teach ethics and values, first of all, by example. When parents or grandparents choose to do the right thing, children will usually follow suit. When they choose to do one thing and try to teach something else, children understand that message as well.

The authors of *Torah With Love* suggest teaching Jewish values through weekly family discussions. All children love a story, and if the story has a moral along with a plot—well, why not? Another helpful book, completely secular in orientation, is *The Kids Book of Questions*. Questions include, "When did you get yourself in the biggest mess by telling a lie? What do you think would have happened if you had just told the truth?" It's great for 9 to 12 year olds; *guaranteed* not to bore the child. The questions will make you stop and think, too.

In a "me first" world, it's essential to teach kids values to live by. As children reach the teen years and begin to resist their parents' rules, encourage them to talk with you. Listen carefully to them and ask them to listen as you tell your side of the issue. A give and take process encourages teens to think about moral conflicts (such as their needs versus their parents' concerns). Teenagers, almost by natural law, resist parental authority. But if you have maintained a warm relationship, they will still value your respect and your approval. You are in a perfect position to reinforce the guidelines laid down by the parents. There's a good chance they'll listen to you rationally, even if they feel it would be "uncool" to acknowledge that the message has struck home.

ANTI-SEMITISM

As a Jewish grandparent and a member of a minority group you have probably faced anti-Semitism in your lifetime. Certain housing developments were off limits, a quota system existed in certain colleges, many industries barred their doors, particularly at management levels. Jews have suffered Pharoah, Haman, the Crusades, pogroms, and finally Hitler. Anti-Semites throughout history have not only opposed Judaism, they have also propounded the belief that Jews are evil.

There may be relatives in your non-Jewish in-law's family who were brought up in narrow or even outright bigoted environments. All you can do where they are concerned is be yourself. Be prepared to answer questions and offer facts that might dispel unfounded prejudices should an appropriate opportunity arise.

Almost inevitably, your grandchild is going to be exposed to anti-Semitism in one form or another. You can play a significant role in how he responds to it. Although anti-Semitism appears to be less blatant than a decade ago, it often lurks just beneath the surface.

Try playing a Jewish values game with your school-age grandchild to see how sensitive he is to certain moral values. Have the child rank the following in terms of their importance to the Jewish people: survival of Israel, Jewish tradition, giving to charity, anti-Semitism, performing a *mitzvah*. You might ask a teenage grandchild for his opinion on the following: a newspaper story about a high school teacher dismissed because of anti-Semitic remarks or cars vandalized outside a synagogue during Friday night services.

The Jewish blood in his veins is a fact; whether he responds to this fact with pride or shame can be significantly influenced by a wise grandparent. The more information you can give your grandchildren to counter the many fallacies on which anti-Semitism is based, the more important you will have proved to be in his development and in his life.

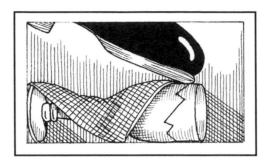

JEWISH CUSTOMS AND SUPERSTITIONS

Your grandchild will enjoy learning about Jewish customs and sayings. Perhaps you are still practicing many of them. Even if you don't do these things yourself, you still probably remember some of the peculiar ones your own grandparents did. Harvey Lupske's *Book of Customs* (see appendix) will give you the information to share on how these customs came about. I can assure you there will be some new ones you'll enjoy.

Did your grandmother tell you to "pull up or down on your ears when you sneeze?" Why? Just do it, you're supposed to! Was it a *bubbameiseh*, an "old wives tale," or did it actually ward off the evil spirits? Whatever way you pull your ears you need to say "*tzu laayngeh mazeldikker yohrn,*" to a long, lucky life. How about the "*pooh*"? Everyone who has seen *Fiddler on the Roof* has heard it. The spitting and saying can be for either good or bad events. When it's good, it's used as a safeguard to keep those selfsame evil spirits at bay. The spitting, the saliva, was considered a potent anti-magic safeguard. Fortunately, the "*pooh*" became symbolic rather than actually spitting, otherwise that particular custom would definitely be really gross.

There are customs like breaking a glass at the wedding ceremony under the foot of the groom that reminds us at a joyous occasion of the destruction of the temple in Jerusalem. Some of the customs have explanations that we can tell about; for others the meaning is hidden, but we do them anyway. Don't forget to wear a safety pin on a trip, so it should bring you good luck. In Judaism, when a rule was uncertain in court, and they were doubtful about the correct decision, the popular custom of the time prevailed.

Sharing such expressions and superstitions with your grandchild will give him great insight into the emotional and ethnic basis of your Jewish life. It all goes under the heading of folklore, and it is folklore that gives ethnicity its color and texture. You owe it to your grandchildren to pass along as much as possible.

Music heard so deeply
That it is not heard at all, but you are the music
While the music lasts.

T.S. Eliot, 1888-1965

MUSIC AND THE JEWISH PEOPLE

When you're sharing your Jewish way of life with your grandchild you need to emphasize that every joyous occasion, every festival and ceremony is celebrated with music. Traditionally, our prayers are not recited, they are chanted, each with its own characteristic intonation. The *kiddush*, the *Kol Nidre*, the blessing over the Chanukah candles—who, once having heard them, can ever forget?

The Sabbath Queen is ushered in with song. On Chanukah the home resounds with songs, and the *Seder* at Passover has its own enchantment. A *Seder* is in fact a perfect setting for stressing a child's Jewish heritage. Children are an integral part of the service. Perhaps, with his parent's permission, your grandchild can learn to chant the Four Questions.

Buy a tape of *klezmer* music and listen together. *Klezmer* is a Jewish folk music with a wonderful beat. Take your grandchild to a live performance when a *klezmer* band comes to your area. Also if the Inbal dance troupe of Israel, which does Yemenite and Chasidic dances, should be in town, get tickets.

Enroll in an Israeli dance class together; you both will have a wonderful experience. If you have the opportunity, take the grandchild to a Jewish wedding so that he can join in with spirited dancing; who doesn't love a *hora*?

Songs make the home even more beautiful. Jewish children through the ages have been nurtured on folk songs sung by their mothers and grandmothers. Now there are new folk songs to sing from Israel. Your grandchild will enjoy learning the songs with you. Don't forget to tell him that "Hatikvah" is the national anthem of Israel; it was adopted as such when Israel became independent in 1948. Explain that "Rock of Ages" (*Maoz Tzur*) tells the exciting tale of Chanukah, of Judah Maccabee and his brave cohorts. You get the idea.

He that hath pity upon the poor lendeth unto the Lord.

Proverbs 19:17

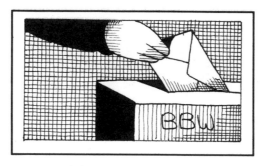

TZEDAKAH

Tzedakah literally means righteousness, but, most commonly, the word is used to signify charity. How do we foster *tzedakah* in our grandchildren? By regularly talking about it, and teaching by example.

The Bible repeatedly exhorts us to give charity to the poor. "If there be among you a needy person, one of your brethren...you must surely open your hand to him...." (Deut. 15:7-8). "Do not harden your heart, nor shut your hand from your needy brother." (Deut. 15:7).

Let the child see you put coins into the *tzedakah* box. Talk about where the coins will go: B'nai B'rith Women, UJA, your synagogue, other worthwhile causes. Discuss the possibility of the child giving a percentage of his allowance for *tzedakah*.

Let him know that you send contributions to honor friends and family members on happy occasions—for the birth of a child, or a wedding or anniversary—and even at sad times like when someone is ill or dies. Along with encouraging him to donate money, engage your grandchild in collecting outgrown clothes and food to give to the needy. Older children can help gather and distribute items for Russian immigrants who settle in the community, give some money to a particular children's home in Israel, or work in a kitchen that delivers food to the needy.

Teach the child early that one of the highest forms of charity is giving anonymously. Why is this so? Because in this way, the recipient is not embarrassed. *Tzedakah* should be given cheerfully and sympathetically. If the child learns this at an early age it will become part of his life. It's one of the most important lessons you can teach him.

This wicked man Hitler, the repository and embodiment of many forms of soul-destroying hatred...

Winston S. Churchill, 1874-1965

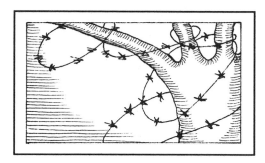

HOLOCAUST

Although most history textbooks give only a paragraph or two to the subject, the Holocaust is a topic all Jewish and non-Jewish children should hear about. Naturally what is told must be appropriate to the age level. Around age five or six a child knows full well what the words good and bad mean. Holocaust Remembrance Day, which usually falls in March or April, (the 27th day of *Nissan* on the Hebrew calendar) is an appropriate time to talk about the Holocaust. Many synagogues, and sometimes even churches, hold services commemorating this day.

Very simply, you can tell the young child that there was a very evil man who wanted to kill all the Jews, and that his name was Hitler. Make sure he knows that Hitler did not succeed in killing *all* the Jews and that he is now dead. Around age 9 or 10 children can be introduced to books about the Holocaust. In their early teens the Holocaust can be discussed in terms of how it affects all Jews, to this very day; perhaps there are people the child may know who were affected personally. When the child is ready for more details he will either ask questions or do his own research. There will be films and, from time to time, TV shows about the Holocaust. If you visit Israel with an older grandchild, *Yad Vashem* will tell it all.

The message you want your grandchild to receive is that Jews are survivors, despite the odds. It reaffirms his faith and his hope for the future.

ISRAEL

On May 14, 1948, Jews throughout the world cheered the birth of the State of Israel with pride and great emotion. A visit to Israel with a grandchild will fill you, too, with great emotion. It's inspirational and fun. It strengthens family bonds. And everyone gets hooked on history. History is literally everywhere; there is more to see, to do, and to learn than can possibly be covered in a single trip. It's a matter of priorities, and planning the trip with your grandchild can't help but draw you closer together before the trip even starts. If it's a first visit, do try to select a good guide or join a group.

But let's face it, trips to Israel are expensive, and if you have more than one grandchild it may not be feasible. The next best thing is teaching your grandchildren everything you can about Israel, how it came to be created, its struggles, its problems, its very reason for being. Talk about its people, the flag, songs, youth, and spirit. The appendix contains excellent, informative, and exciting material for all ages. In addition, you can check out videotapes of such movies as *Exodus*, *Cast a Giant Shadow*, and *Raid on Entebbe* that instruct while they entertain.

More than kisses, letters mingle souls; for thus friends absent speak.

John Donne, 1572-1631

LOVE LETTERS FROM GRANDPARENTS

Letter writing is a forgotten art. Who bothers anymore? In our youth, no one called long distance unless there was a death in the family. Now, we call across the country as casually as we call across the street.

But letters are special. Simply because they take time and careful thought, they prove to the recipient that you care.

Love letters from grandparents are designed to strengthen the relationship between grandparents and grandchildren who are separated by distance. By using the mail to share their thoughts and experiences, grandparents and grandchildren will draw closer together, learn from each other, and build a reservoir of happy memories. Every child loves receiving mail. It makes him feel special and important. And letters can be saved and read again and again. Don't you have a box of letters you've been saving for years?

With a younger child keep the letters simple. Let him know you will send him special letters giving stories about your own life. Ask him to keep the letters and pictures you send him in a scrapbook. You can even send him the scrapbook! Send return envelopes with a stamp affixed and you'll get a quicker reply.

Letters may be handwritten, typed, or taped on a tape recorder. I still have a personal preference for the handwritten letter, but if your writing is like mine, perhaps typing is better. The correspondence should take place every two or three weeks, even if only a postcard. Imagine a grandchild as a grown-up reading your letters and feeling close to you, even after you are gone.

Children like to be told you care. Let them know how much they are missed if you don't see them often. A letter that tells them how great you think they are will be pulled out and read when they feel stressed or depressed. It's great for a person to know, no matter what, that he can depend on this unconditional love.

And don't forget letters to grandchildren away at college or camp where they miss family and home life. There may be some stresses that they can discuss with you because you have been a good sounding board and are not judgmental, things that they can't discuss with their own parents. This is a golden opportunity to keep the relationship strong.

Why did Moses wander in the desert for 40 years before bringing the Jews out? Because like most men he wouldn't ask for directions.

Anonymous

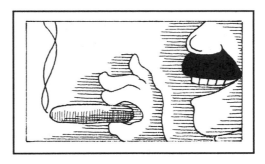

JEWISH WIT AND HUMOR

Laughter and the ability to joke and poke fun at themselves have helped Jews survive many crises. As my own mother grows older she often says, "I know as I age, I will lose many of my faculties, but please Lord, let my sense of humor be the last to go."

Jewish wit and humor have endured for some 35 centuries. The Torah is full of humor and riddles. Freud was particularly impressed with the degree to which Jews were willing to joke about their shortcomings. Jewish humor has an edge to it, and as often as not, is self-deprecating. Jewish humor has its own special flavor. Yiddish jokes sound funny even if you don't understand a word. Now *that's* humor!

Jews have a propensity to hurl honey-coated barbs at those nearest and dearest to their hearts. On cassettes, Mickey Katz is a master of musical mischief with his "Borscht Riders in the Sky" and "Bagel Call Rag." Michael Rosenberg's "Getzel at the Baseball Game" has hilarious monologues in Yinglish. Billy Hodes cassette of 20th century Yiddish humor gives contributions from Myron Cohen and George Jessel. On video and television, you can enjoy the humor of Joan Rivers, Roseanne Barr Arnold, Billy Crystal, Jackie Mason, George Burns, and Woody Allen. You and your grandchild will have great fun laughing at the *mishegaas* (craziness) of these and other Jewish comedians.

61

DEATH AND THE SHIVA PERIOD

Death is frightening to a child. It's frightening to all of us. But there are specific Jewish ways to deal with this stark fact of human existence, and the traditions have been well thought out. It can be explained to the child that the casket is made entirely of wood, without nails, in keeping with the precept "ashes to ashes, dust to dust." The wood will ultimately disintegrate; metal can be permanent.

After the funeral, friends call and provide the meal so that the mourners need not be distracted. During *shiva*, friends call. It is an important *mitzvah*. It helps the mourners through the first traumatic days and gives them solace and support. A memorial candle will burn in the home for the entire seven days of the *shiva* period if the family is Orthodox. The custom varies by family and by circumstance.

The *Kaddish* prayer can be explained in detail—what it means, when it is said, why it is said. *Yahrzeit* too can be explained. Even non-observant Jews find themselves back in the synagogue or temple for the *yahrzeit* of their parents. There are many Jewish traditions and customs surrounding this most awesome of events. Each of them have profound reasons and moral implications. The death of someone close is a sobering experience for all of us. The Jewish manner of dealing with it is very special and meaningful, and that meaning should be conveyed in full.

During a family member's *yahrzeit*, take your grandchild to visit a Jewish cemetery if the parents have no objection. It is a sign of respect to visit the graves of loved ones. Do a tombstone rubbing for the family history collection. Explain (if you are able) what is written in Hebrew on the tombstone. Children, as well as adults, have a difficult time understanding death. The grandparent, through discussion and books, can help the child better understand the life cycle. A visit to a cemetery, especially when tied to a special time, is not macabre; it is a moving and meaningful experience. One young man of 20 said to me at the funeral of his 90-year-old grandfather, "No matter what I did or what I wore, and I wore some strange clothes at one time, my grandfather always told me he loved me. He was the shining beacon of my life."

MARRIAGE AND YOUR GRANDCHILD

Your own children made their choice. Now your granddaughter is coming over to talk about her choice of marriage partner. Imagine that! That little girl, your *granddaughter*, speaking seriously of marriage. Where have the years gone?

She assures you she has found her own "true love" but wouldn't mind some advice. Wonder of wonders! Her *mother* never asked you for advice! When she comes over, you tell her that there is an old legend that 40 days before a Jewish child is born, its mate is selected in heaven. (When you see the mate, sometimes you can't help but think that heaven has an odd sense of humor.) She may not have heard about the *shadkhen* (matchmaker), as it went out of fashion even before your generation. But the *shadkhen* tried to match family standing and pedigree, weighing individual qualities that might strengthen compatibility.

Whether her young man is Jewish or non-Jewish, recommend that she discuss religion with her intended and try to come to a meeting of the minds. If their views are too far apart, there may be serious trouble in the future, so the time to tackle the issue is now. Urge her to be mindful of how important it is to share common interests and to be respectful of each other's backgrounds and possible differences. If this is to be an interfaith marriage, it is important to stress that it usually works out better if the children are raised in one religion, with information about the cultural roots of the other. If, indeed, he is her "true love," you will not change her mind. As you have always done in the past, give her your blessing and prayers for her happiness.

Immortality is not a gift. Immortality is an achievement, and only those who strive mightily shall possess it.

Edgar Lee Masters, 1869-1950

ETHICAL WILL

As we young grandparents begin to age, we start thinking of what we are going to leave our grandchildren. Speaking candidly, the thoughts we most often have are rather selfish. How will they remember us? Will we soon be forgotten, or will they cling to good thoughts of us all of their lives? Writing an ethical will is one way to address the issue of how we will be remembered. It is an old Jewish custom going back to biblical times. Moses in the Book of Deuteronomy left an ethical will giving his people guidelines on how to live.

In your last will and testament you distribute your material things. In an ethical will you try to sum up what you have learned in life and what you want for your children. The writer searches for the essence of what deserves to be passed along. The writing process itself compels self-examination. You force yourself to contemplate what is truly important. You leave no doubt as to your thoughts for your children's future. (See appendix for book on ethical wills.)

Putting down who you are and what values you want to pass on is no easy task, especially if you are completely honest. And the ethical will is meaningless without honesty. Pious platitudes are strictly forbidden.

In his ethical will, Mike Moldeven of Del Mar, California, wrote: "I've come to accept that there must be a Purpose to our universe, and therefore Purpose to we who are of its essence. To me, being without Purpose is to be without meaning...all of life, all of us, would be meaningless. I hope each of you will also accept that life has meaning and guide yourselves accordingly. Live together in harmony. Think of the family when issues surface which might create dissension among you. Help each other in times of need even though you might live great distances apart and your lifestyles differ. Carry the family heritage with dignity. Try not to discard customs and rituals you consider trivial; bear in mind that many have come down centuries and have withstood the test of fire."

Carefully and honestly crafted, your ethical will can be a treasure for generations to come.

PART V
SPECIAL
SECTION

Couples are wholes and not wholes, what agrees disagrees, the concordant is discordant. From all things one and from one all things.

Heraclitus, c. 540 - c. 480 B.C.E.

FAMILY DIFFERENCES

What Heraclitus was trying to say is that families can be strange. And that goes for all sorts of families.

Around the age of five a child will begin perceiving family differences.

Divorce is a word that is becoming part of a young child's vocabulary. It is not uncommon for very young children to ask their parents if they are going to get a divorce when they hear them arguing. Many of their playmates are from divorced families. Divorce in Jewish families has been escalating. Usually children have lots of sad feelings when they are living in single-parent homes. They may be scared, worried, embarrassed, and thoroughly mixed-up. Sometimes mom or dad have remarried and they have stepparents, several sets of grandparents, stepbrothers and sisters, and a whole array of aunts and uncles. The considerable emotional turmoil increases when they have to cope with different cultures and faiths as well. It's bewildering enough for an adult to sort out, let alone a child.

As a grandparent you can be a security blanket for your grandchild while he or she is trying to cope with the changes and feelings brought about by divorce. At this difficult time, a grandchild needs reassurance of your love and as much contact as possible. If you can't be there in person, be sure you call and write frequently. You might also want to send him such books as *Who Will Lead The Kiddush?* (see appendix), and *Dinosaurs Divorce* (see appendix). These books will help him get through this difficult time.

Let there be no strife, I pray thee, between me and thee...for we are brethren.

Genesis 13:8

BLENDED ROOTS

You may have step-grandchildren that are of several different religions, especially if there has been a second marriage. The most mingled example I've run across is the situation of one young couple with whom I spoke. The wife is Catholic, the husband is Jewish, and she has four married sisters. One had married a convert to Catholicism, one married a Quaker, one a Lutheran, and one an agnostic. By the time this girl came home with her Jewish fiance, her mother just shrugged and said "big deal."

It is difficult not to favor your own grandchild over the grandchildren acquired through a child's marriage. Let's be honest. It's impossible. But make a conscious, superhuman effort not to let it show. You will earn a huge number of brownie points and from time to time you're going to need them. Just remember *these are all your grandchildren.*

Even more of a challenge arises when your grandchildren live in homes where dual religions are celebrated and a church and synagogue are alternately attended. It would be easier if one religion had been adopted, but that's not your call. How can you help your grandchildren and step-grandchildren learn to respect and enjoy these differences?

This is the time to reinforce the concept that we all pray to one God, want to do what's right and to help our neighbor. It is particularly important to reinforce the idea that all religions strive to make us better human beings, to live right and to do right. Explain that different cultures in different countries led to different modes of religious expression.

How do you explain your belief in your own religion without, by inference, casting a negative aspersion on another? You don't. You can only state firmly and honestly who *you* are and what *you* believe. You can and should let your grandchild know that there are others who believe differently, and that their beliefs must be respected (nobody said this was easy!). But without disparaging another faith, you can—you should—make clear where you stand. Unless your own commitment to your Jewish heritage rings true, what chance can you possibly have to truly share your love for Judaism with your grandchild?

Opinion is ultimately determined by the feelings, and not by the intellect.
Herbert Spencer, 1820-1903

DUAL FAITHS

There are many stresses and worries in households where family members have different backgrounds, languages, customs, foods and religious values; where mother and father may celebrate different holidays. Whether Jew or non-Jew, a grandparent can help the grandchild living in this situation learn to respect and cope with the differences.

As our opening quote so aptly states, while we think things through as logically and rationally as we can, we tend to *act* on the basis of our instincts, our feelings. Most of the time these turn out to be right.

When you talk with your grandchildren, do a lot of listening and try to let the child know that he can tell you how he feels. Try to explain that feelings aren't good or bad, they just are. Encourage him to express his true feelings openly, even when he thinks they are "bad." Feelings are honest but not always honestly expressed. A close, warm, non-judgmental relationship can be a true anchor for a child caught up in an insecure situation.

Make certain the child feels free to call you at any time. If you live out of town, check into the personal 800 number now offered by some long distance phone companies. With this service, your grandchild's call will be billed to you rather than to his parents.

As an unintended bonus, the close bond you forge with this grandchild will, by extension, help create a positive perception of things Jewish. (You, after all, are the "Jewish grandparent.") That, of course, has no bearing on your fervent wish to help your grandchild through difficult times. It is simply a good by-product from a bad situation.

Children of interfaith marriage sometimes find themselves looking at every issue as if they had dual personalities. Even when there has been a conversion of one parent, differences in cultural and ethnic identity remain. Where there has been no choice of religion on the part of the parents, or if the choice has been left up to the child, your grandchild may, as an adult, feel like an outsider in both the Jewish and Christian worlds. Who are his friends? What holidays will he celebrate? With whom does he "really" belong?

If, as a grandparent, you have developed a good relationship and have kept the communication going, you can now be a much needed sounding board for your grandchild as he tries to sort out his emotional turmoil. Almost inevitably there will be radical swings in perception—one day he will see things one way, the next another. Don't be startled or disappointed if, after apparently opting for a Jewish orientation, he should change his mind. He is going to have a lifetime of internal debate, with circumstances constantly altering outcomes.

Ideally, with you as a good role model, his Jewish heritage will help him make a choice that will let him find peace and a fulfilling identity.

Religion, of which the rewards are distant, and which is animated only by faith and hope, will glide by degrees out of the mind unless it be invigorated and reimpressed by...the salutary influence of example.

Samuel Johnson, 1709-1784

LONG DISTANCE GRANDPARENTING

Samuel Johnson had it right. Without a committed example as a guide, children quickly perceive that religion is just being given lip service. What's a grandparent to do, particularly one who's out of town and only gets to see the kids once or twice a year?

Developing a close relationship with your grandchildren isn't easy. It takes hard work, but it pays big dividends. When you live many miles away and see your little ones infrequently, it's easy for them to forget you. The brief telephone calls aren't too satisfying, especially when children are young and don't always want to come to the telephone. And even with the greatest effort and will you can muster, realistically, you only have limited influence and impact. But that doesn't mean you won't have any influence at all, particularly if you really try.

There are five ways I find to make the worthwhile connections: letters, photographs, telephone calls, cassette and videotapes, and gifts. One of the most effective ways to connect is through the camcorder. We made videos of my father *olav hasholom* at Passover before he passed away. Our grandchildren (his great-grandchildren) who were born after he died feel they knew him because they have seen the tapes and heard his voice. These tapes, like books, will be kept and passed down.

One of the most important events in a child's life is his birthday. When you can't be there in person, at least send a make-believe tape pretending you are there helping him celebrate. You don't have to own a camcorder—there's usually someone to borrow one from and if not, rent one. The more thought you give to making the tape and the more props you use, the more he will enjoy it. And if there are other relatives in town (particularly cousins of like age), get them all into the act. It may not be optioned for a sitcom, but it will be a guaranteed smash with your grandchild. Along with the tape, be sure to send some balloons and party hats.

Introducing yourself to a distant grandchild through letters takes some initial groundwork. Tell your grandchild you would really like to get to know him and to let him know about you. Tried and true openers, either written or taped, include variations of "I remember when...." "Let me tell you about the time we...." "There was the time your mom/dad and I went to see...." Sending a photo along, tour maps or brochures, even your own sketches will give the personal touch. In turn, ask the child to tell you about a pet, school, favorite sport, favorite holiday, good deeds, favorite foods, and T.V. shows. Ask questions such as: If you had a lot of money what would you buy? If you could be anyone for a day who would you like to be? As you get to know the child you can get into more serious topics.

Holidays are difficult when families can't be together. But, you can let your far-away grandchildren know you miss them by sharing some of the family traditions with them via camcorder. Tape part of the *Seder* and holiday celebrations and send the tape in a special holiday box along with books about the holiday and some significant edibles. It's not nearly the same as having the family with you, but at least you have given them a part of yourself. (See script in appendix.)

Whoever teaches his son teaches not only his son but also his son's, and so on to the end of generations.

Talmud: Kiddushin 30a

A FINAL THOUGHT

Considering the wide range of topics discussed, and the range of viewpoints there are among individuals, certainly you may not agree with some of what I have written.

But consider this. If, in the entire book, you have picked up even one new idea that is useful, it has been more than worthwhile reading through to the very end.

And don't think just because you're finished with the book you're through. The appendix is a treasure-trove of enormously useful information.

In interviews with rabbis, priests, and ministers, I always ask the same question, "If you could leave three gifts to an interfaith grandchild, what would they be?" The answer from all of them is essentially the same:

1. A sense of identity
2. Life's ethical values
3. Spirituality and social responsibility

This sums up the theologians. Not surprisingly, grandparents themselves give much the same answers.

A close relationship with your grandchild will make it much easier for you to bring Jewish traditions and heritage to life for that child. In the process, you may encourage him to identify with you and with Judaism. At the very least, you will help your grandchild find more meaning in his or her life. Give it an honest try.

RESOURCES FOR GRANDPARENTS

(FOR BETTER UNDERSTANDING OF INTERFAITH COUPLES)

Cowan, Rachel & Paul. *Mixed Blessings.* Doubleday, New York, 1987.

Guzen, Lee F. *Raising Your Jewish/Christian Child: How Interfaith Parents Can Give Children the Best of Both Their Heritages.* Newmarket Press, New York, 1990.

Petsonk, Judy and Remsen, Jim. *The Intermarriage Handbook: A Guide for Jews and Christians.* Arbor House/William Morrow Company, New York, 1988.

Reuben, Rabbi Steven Carr. *But How Will You Raise the Children? A Guide to Interfaith Marriage.* Pocket Books/Simon & Schuster, New York, 1987.

Romanoff, Lena. *Your People, My People.* Jewish Publication Society, Philadelphia, 1990.

Schneider, Susan Weidman. *Intermarriage: The Challenge of Living With Differences Between Christians & Jews.* Free Press, New York, 1989.

FURTHER READING

Donin, Rabbi Hayim. *To Raise a Jewish Child.* Basic Books, New York, 1977.

Epstein, David and Stutman, Susan Singer. *Torah With Love.* Prentice Hall, New York, 1986.

Gubbay, Lucien and Levy, Abraham. *The Jewish Book of Why & What.* Shapolsky Press, New York, 1989.

Heller, David. *Talking to Your Child about God.* Bantam, New York, 1988.

Lutske, Harvey. *Book of Jewish Customs.* Jason Aronson, Inc., Northvale, New Jersey, 1986.

Novak, William and Waldoks, Moshe. *The Big Book of Jewish Humor.* Harper & Row, New York, 1981.

Renberg, Dalia. *The Complete Family Guide to Jewish Holidays.* Adama Books, Bellmore, New York, 1985.

Singer, Rabbi Shmuel. *A Parent's Guide To Teaching Children Mitzvot.* KTAV Publishing, Hoboken, New Jersey, 1991.

Stampfer, Nathaniel. *Ethical Wills: A Modern Treasury.* Schocken Books, New York, 1983.

Tabachnik, Joseph, and Forster, Brenda. *Jews By Choice.* KTAV Publications, Hoboken, New Jersey, 1991.

Telushkin, Rabbi Joseph. *Jewish Literacy.* William Morrow & Co., New York, 1990.

BOOKS FOR GRANDCHILDREN

A love for reading can be a special gift a grandparent can impart to a grandchild. The following are books to teach the Jewish way of life: workbooks, crafts and games (w); books dealing with interfaith topics (i).

JEWISH IDENTITY

PRESCHOOL 2-5 YEARS

Aranow, Sarah. *Seven Days of Creation.* Shapolsky Press, Inc., New York, 1985.

Bogot, Howard I. and Syme, Daniel B. *Books Are Treasures.* UAHC Press, New York, 1982.

Brinn, Ruth Esrig. *Let's Celebrate.* (w) Kar-Ben Press, Rockville, Maryland, 1978.

Goldstein, Andrew. *My Very Own Jewish Home.* Kar-Ben Press, Rockville, Maryland, 1983.

Greenberg, Melanie Hope. *Celebrations, Our Jewish Holidays.* Jewish Publication Society, Philadelphia, 1991.

Levy, Eugene. *How We Celebrate.* (w)(i) UAHC Press, New York, 1990.

Syme, Deborah Shayne. *The Jewish Home Detectives.* UAHC Press, New York, 1981.

SCHOOL AGE 5-8 YEARS

Adler, David A. *Jewish Holiday Fun.* (w) Kar-Ben Press, Rockville, Maryland, 1987.

Cederbaum, Sophie N. *First Book of Jewish Holidays.* UAHC, New York, 1987.

Feder, Harriet K. *Judah Who Always Said No.* Kar-Ben Press, Rockville, Maryland, 1990.

Goldstein, Sandy. *There's No Such Thing as a Chanukah Bush.* (i) Albert Whitman & Co., Morton Grove, Illinois, 1983.

Pliskin, Jacqueline. *The Bible Story Activity Book.* (w) Shapolsky Press, New York, 1990.

Pomerantz, Barbara. *Who Will Lead the Kiddush?* UAHC, New York, 1985.

Polacco, Patricia. *The Keeping Quilt.* Simon & Schuster, New York, 1988.

Portnoy, Mindy. *Mommy Never Went To Hebrew School.* (i) Kar-Ben Press, Rockville, Maryland, 1989.

Pushker, Gloria Teles. *Toby Belfer Never Had a Christmas Tree.* (i) Pelican Press, Gretna, Louisiana, 1991.

Roseman, Kenneth. *All in a Jewish Family.* UAHC, New York, 1984.

Stern, Rabbi Jack. *Gates of Awe: Holy Day Prayers for Young Children.* Central Conference of American Rabbis, New York, 1991.

Stock, Gregory. *The Kids Book of Questions.* Workman Publishers, New York, 1988.

INTERMEDIATE (9-12) YEARS

Bogot, Howard I. and Kipper, Lenore. *The Alef Bet of Jewish Values.* UAHC, New York, 1990.

Burstein, Chaya. *The Jewish Kids Catalog.* Jewish Publication Society, Philadelphia, 1985.

Chaikin, Miriam. *Hanukah.* Holiday House, New York, 1990.

Cohen, Barbara. *The Secret Grove.* UAHC, New York, 1985.

Cowan, Paul. *A Torah Is Written.* Jewish Publication Society, Philadelphia, 1990.

Gallant, Janet. *My Brother's Bar Mitzvah.* Kar-Ben Press, Rockville, Maryland, 1990.

Pliskin, Jacqueline Jacobsen. *Jewish Holiday Games.* (w) Shapolsky Press, New York, 1990.

Hurwitz, Johanna. *Once I Was a Plum Tree.* (i) William Morrow & Company, New York, 1980.

Isaacs, Ronald. *The Jewish Family Game Book for Sabbath and Other Festivals.* KTAV, Hoboken, New Jersey, 1989.

JUNIOR HIGH

Barrie, Barbara. *Lone Star.* (i) Delacorte Press (Bantam Dell), New York, 1990.

Bush, Lawrence. *Emma Ansky-Levine & Her Mitzvah Machine.* UAHC, New York, 1991

Bush, Lawrence. *Rooftop Secrets and Other Stories of Anti-Semitism.* UAHC, New York, 1987.

Blume, Judy. *Are You There God? It's Me, Margaret.* (i) Dell Publishing, New York, 1974.

Cohen, Barbara. *King Of The Seventh Grade.* (i) William Morrow, New York, 1982.

Perlmutter, Philip. *Jewish Nobel Prizewinners.* (w) KTAV, Hoboken, New Jersey, 1989.

Sherman, Eileen Bluestone. *Independence Avenue.* Jewish Publication Society, Philadelphia, 1990.

SENIOR HIGH

Brody, Seymour. *Jewish Heroes of America.* Shapolsky Press, New York, 1991.

Cohen, Henry. *Why Judaism?* UAHC, New York, 1989.

Gordon, Sol. *When Living Hurts: For Teenagers and Young Adults.* UAHC, New York, 1985.

Lynn, Erwin. *A Jewish Baseball Hall of Fame.* Shapolsky Press, New York, 1987.

Postal, Bernard and Koppman, Lionel. *Guess Who's Jewish in American History.* Shapolsky Press, New York, 1985.

Rottenberg, Dan. *Guide Book To Jewish Genealogy.* Genealogy Publications, Baltimore, 1986.

COLLEGE AND ADULT

Belth, Nathan. *A Promise To Keep: The American Encounter with Anti-Semitism.* Shapolsky Press, New York, 1988.

Goldberg, Drs. Lee & Lana. *The Jewish Student's Guide to American Colleges.* Shapolsky Press, New York, 1989.

Goodman-Malamuth, Leslie and Margolis, Robin. *Between Two Worlds: Choices for Grown Children of Jewish-Christian Parents.* Pocket Books/Simon and Schuster, New York, 1992.

Kukoff, Lydia. *Choosing Judaism.* UAHC, New York, 1981.

Shapiro, Mark. *Gates of Shabbat: A Guide for Observing Shabbat.* Central Conference of American Rabbis, New York, 1991.

Siegel, Richard and Strassfeld, Michael and Sharon. *The First Jewish Catalog.* Jewish Publication Society, Philadelphia, 1988.

Strassfeld, Michael & Sharon. *The Second Jewish Catalog.* Jewish Publication Society, Philadelphia, 1989.

Syme, Daniel. *The Jewish Home.* UAHC, New York, 1989.

ISRAEL
AGES 5-8

Adler, David A. *A Picture Book Of Israel.* Holiday House, New York, 1984.

Burstein, Chaya. *What's An Israel.* (w) Kar-Ben Press, Rockville, Maryland, 1983.

Carmi, Giora. *And Shira Imagined.* Jewish Publication Society, Philadelphia, 1988.

Grand, Samuel & Tamar. *The Children of Israel.* UAHC, New York, 1972.

Topek, Susan Remick. *Israel Is (Ages 1-4).* Kar-Ben Press, Rockville, Maryland, 1989.

AGES 9-12

Burstein, Chaya. *A Kid's Catalog of Israel.* Jewish Publication Society, Philadelphia, 1988.

Sidon, Ephraim. *The Animated Israel.* Shapolsky Press, New York, 1988.

Sofer, Barbara. *Kids Love Israel, Israel Loves Kids.* Kar-Ben Press, Rockville, Maryland, 1988.

AGES 13-16

Davidson, Margaret. *The Golda Meir Story.* Charles Scribner's Sons, New York, 1976.

Rabinovich, Abraham. *The Battle for Jerusalem.* Jewish Publication Society, Philadelphia, 1987.

Seymour, Rossel. *Israel: Covenant People, Covenant Land.* UAHC, New York, 1989.

ADULT

Millgram, Abraham E., *Jerusalem Curiosities.* Jewish Publication Society, Philadelphia, 1989.

Rubinger, David. *Witness To An Era: 40 Years of Photographs of Israel.* Shapolsky Press, New York, 1989.

HOLOCAUST
AGES 5-8

Adler, David. *Number On My Grandfather's Arm.* UAHC, New York, 1987.

Ginsburg, Marvell. *Tattoed Torah.* UAHC, New York, 1989.

AGES 9-12

Hurwitz, Johanna. *Anne Frank: A Life In Hiding.* Jewish Publication Society, Philadelphia, 1988.

Provost, Gary and Gail. *David and Max.* Jewish Publication Society, Philadelphia, 1990.

Roseman, Kenneth. *Escape From the Holocaust.* UAHC, New York, 1989.

AGES 13-16

Adler, David. *We Remember the Holocaust.* Holt & Co., New York, 1989.

Gray, Ronald. *Hitler and the Germans.* Lerner, Minneapolis, Minnesota, 1983.

Wolff, Marion Freyer. *The Shrinking Circle.* UAHC, New York, 1990.

ADULT

Maza, Bernard. *With Fury Poured Out.* Shapolsky Press, New York, 1989.

Cohn-Sherbock, Dan. *Holocaust Theology.* Harper, San Francisco, 1989.

Meltzer, Milton. *Never To Forget: The Jews of the Holocaust.* Harper and Row, New York, 1976.

APPENDIX
MAKE BELIEVE SCRIPT FOR CHANUKAH
FOR AUDIO TAPE OR VIDEO
(AGES 3-6 YEARS)

Hello (child's name). This is (grandparent's name). I'm sorry I'm not going to be with you in person for Chanukah. I think about you every day and miss you so much. This tape will be like a visit with you. We had so much fun the last time we were together. This tape will tell you how much I love you. I wish I could be there to hug you. I'm sending you a Chanukah surprise box filled with packages that you can enjoy and think of (grandparent's name).

Ready, open the *big* box and take out the package that has a #1 on it. Open it up and take out the book that is inside. I'm going to read you the book, *Judah Who Always Said No* (Kar-Ben Press). There is also a glove puppet in the box that you can use while you hear the story. (The glove puppet can be purchased or the child can use magic markers to draw Mattathias on the back, King Antiochus on the front and the five brave Maccabbee brothers a face on each finger. You can draw simple faces that can be colored. If you videotape the script, show the child how to use the puppet.) I hope (grandchild's name) you like the story.

Now, open package #2. There is a Chanukah tape with songs. Put the tape on your recorder and we can practice the songs together - "I Have A Little Dreidel," etc.

Are you ready for the next package? Open #3. I'm going to teach you how to play the *dreidel* game. When the brave Jewish men were told not to pray or study they pretended to play dreidel when the soldiers came around - but they were really studying Torah. Here's how you play. There are four Hebrew letters on the dreidel, *Nun* means nothing, *Gimel* means you get everything in the pot. *Shin* means put in the pot and *Heh* means take one-half of what is in the pot. Hold the dreidel by the top and give it a good spin. What letter is on top? You can practice till you can play with some of your friends or mommy or dad. Use pennies or poker chips and see who wins.

Now it's time to open package #4. There is a menorah so you can light the candles each of the eight nights and remember the miracle of the oil. When you light the candles you say a blessing; *Barach ata Adonai, Eloheynu Melech ha'olam, Asher Kidshanu be'mitzvotav ve'tzivanu le'hadlik ner shel Chanukah.*

Open package #5 very carefully. Don't shake it, it might break. I made you some Chanukah cookies. And look into the package. There are some cookie cutters, a Jewish Star, a Dreidel. Now you can make some more cookies with Mommy. I put my favorite recipe in for you to use. When your (Mom or Dad) was little, we made Chanukah cookies together. I also put in my recipe for potato *latkes.* I didn't think they would go through the mail very well.

I put in some construction paper, paint and patterns for you to make some Chanukah decorations. I hope you have fun. Please take some pictures so I can see you making the Chanukah cookies. I'll watch my mailbox for when you send them to me. I miss you and I hope we get to see you soon.

Bye (child's name). I love you (grandparent's name).

B'NAI B'RITH WOMEN'S MISSION AND GOALS

B'nai B'rith Women's mission to support Jewish women in their families, in their communities and in society has spurred many community service projects in the U.S. and Canada. Just a few of these projects are: conferences on interfaith marriage; outreach to battered women; and educational programs to prevent drug and alcohol abuse among children and adolescents.

BBW's goals are:
- To strengthen the effectiveness of women in improving the quality of life for themselves, their families and society;
- To foster the emotional well-being of children and youth; and
- To perpetuate Jewish life and values.

If you would like to learn more about what BBW is doing in your community, or want information on how to become a member, please write or call:

B'nai B'rith Women
1828 L Street, N.W.
Suite 250
Washington, D.C. 20036
1-800-BBW-4664

B'NAI B'RITH WOMEN
UNITING JEWISH WOMEN